Something To Think About

For Christmastime and Winter Days

Daily Reflections by

Mary Penich
http://MaryPenich.com

Title Page Drawing by
Timothy M. Penich;
used with permission.

Something To Think About...
for Christmastime and Winter Days
©Copyright 2011 by Mary Penich

All rights reserved. No part of this book shall be reproduced, stored in a retrieval system, or transmitted by any means, electronic, mechanical, photocopying or otherwise without prior written permission from the publisher -except for brief quotations in printed reviews. No patent liability is assumed with respect to the use of information herein. Although every precaution has been taken in the preparation of this book, the publisher and the author assume no responsibility for errors or omissions, or for damages resulting from the use of information herein.

Warning and Disclaimer
Every effort mentioned in this book is complete and as accurate as possible. However, no warranty or fitness is implied. The information provided is on an "as is" basis. The author and the publisher have neither liability nor responsibility to any person or entity with respect to any loss or damages arising from the information contained in this book.

For additional copies see:
Amazon.com &
MaryPenich.com

DEDICATION

For God who loves us...

You never cease to amaze me
with the creative and loving ways
in which You are present
to each one of us.
Your ongoing care and inspiration
are constant blessings.
When life is easy and
when life seems unbearable,
You give meaning to our every breath.

for Christmastime and Winter Days

Table of Contents

A NOTE FROM THE AUTHOR..5

Our Journey Together...7

The First Sunday of Advent..9

Monday, the First Week of Advent.......................................13

Tuesday, the First Week of Advent......................................14

Wednesday, the First Week of Advent................................15

Thursday, the First Week of Advent....................................16

Friday, the First Week of Advent..17

Saturday, the First Week of Advent.....................................18

The Second Sunday of Advent..19

Monday, the Second Week of Advent.................................23

Tuesday, the Second Week of Advent.................................24

Wednesday, the Second Week of Advent...........................25

Thursday, the Second Week of Advent...............................26

Friday, the Second Week of Advent.....................................27

Saturday, the Second Week of Advent................................28

The Third Sunday of Advent...29

Monday, the Third Week of Advent....................................33

Tuesday, the Third Week of Advent....................................34

Wednesday, the Third Week of Advent..............................35

Thursday, the Third Week of Advent..................................36

Friday, the Third Week of Advent..37

Saturday, the Third Week of Advent...................................38

The Fourth Sunday of Advent...39

Monday, the Fourth Week of Advent..................................43

Something To Think About...

Tuesday, the Fourth Week of Advent..................................44

Wednesday, the Fourth Week of Advent............................45

Thursday, the Fourth Week of Advent................................46

Friday, the Fourth Week of Advent......................................47

Christmas Eve..48

Christmas Day..49

The Feast of St. Stephen - December 26............................52

The Feast of St. John - December 27..................................53

The Feast of the Holy Innocents - December 28..............54

The Fifth Day of Christmas - December 29........................55

The Sixth Day of Christmas - December 30......................56

The Seventh Day of Christmas - December 31.................57

The Feast of the Holy Family - January 1..........................58

The Ninth Day of Christmas - January 2 62

The Tenth Day of Christmas - January 3 63

The Eleventh Day of Christmas - January 4......................64

The Twelfth Day of Christmas - January 5........................65

Christmas Weekday - January 6 66

Christmas Weekday - January 7 67

The Feast of the Epiphany - January 8...............................68

Monday After the Epiphany - January 9 71

Tuesday After the Epiphany - January 10 72

Wednesday After the Epiphany - January 11....................73

Thursday After the Epiphany - January 12........................74

Friday After the Epiphany - January 13 75

Saturday After the Epiphany - January 14........................76

The Baptism of the Lord - January 15 77

for Christmastime and Winter Days

Monday - January 16 81

Tuesday - January 17, Feast of St. Anthony, Abbot..................82

Wednesday - January 18 83

Thursday - January 19 84

Friday - January 20, St. Fabian and St. Sebastian....................85

Saturday - January 21, Feast of St. Agnes................................86

Second Sunday - January 22 87

Monday - January 23 91

Tuesday - January 24, Feast of St. Francis de Sales................92

Wednesday - January 25, Conversion of St. Paul.....................93

Thursday - January 26, Feast St. Timothy and St. Titus..........94

Friday - January 27, Feast of St. Angela Merici........................95

Saturday - January 28, Feast of St. Thomas Aquinas...............96

The Third Sunday - January 29...97

Monday - January 30..101

Tuesday - January 31, Feast of St. John Bosco......................102

Wednesday - February 1..103

Thursday - February 2, The Presentation of the Lord............104

Friday - February 3, St. Blaise and St. Ansgar.......................105

Saturday - February 4..106

The Fourth Sunday - February 5...107

Monday - February 6, St. Paul Miki and Companions.............111

Tuesday - February 7...112

Wednesday - February 8, St. Jerome and St. Josephine.........113

Thursday - February 9 114

Friday - February 10, St. Scholastica......................................115

Saturday - February 11, Our Lady of Lourdes.........................116

Something To Think About...

The Fifth Sunday - February 12...117

Monday - February 13...121

Tuesday - February 14, St. Cyril and Methodius.....................122

Wednesday - February 15..123

Thursday - February 16...124

Friday - February 17, The Seven Servite Founders..................125

Saturday - February 18..126

The Sixth Sunday - February 19..127

Monday - February 20...131

Tuesday - February 21, St. Peter Damian..................................132

Our Journey Continues...133

A NOTE FROM THE AUTHOR

My affection for the Christmas Season compels me to keep the Spirit alive for as long as I can throughout each New Year. During 2010, this effort included a book of daily devotionals for Lent. I hoped to inspire my readers to become as personally involved with and passionate regarding their Lenten journeys and the promises of Easter as they are about the wonder of Christmas. I will admit to succeeding to at least some degree. When Easter arrived and my daily reflections ran out, many readers acknowledged that they wanted more. This book is my response to their request.

I offer this book to you as an invitation of sorts. I invite you to consider our marvelous Creator who set life as we know it in motion. It doesn't matter much to me whether this loving act began with the Big Bang, Creation according to Genesis or some other means. What does matter to me is that the universe around us is a reflection of the Everlasting's propensity to love. The Source of Life could no more hold love within than I can refrain from showing affection to my little granddaughters. Though humankind systematically rebuffs God's presence among us and within us, God remains constant in loving us. So it is that I invite you to join me in returning this amazing love every moment of every day of our lives.

The reflections I offer are drawn from the life God has so generously bestowed upon me and those who inhabit this earth with me. I hope that this walk through Advent, the Christmas Season and the onset of the New Year will help you to acknowledge God's presence in your own life.

Something To Think About...

If you're concerned that you're not a particularly spiritual person, don't worry. Whether you've come to this realization or not, you are indeed a spiritual being because you were created as such. I've discovered through the joyful, the sorrowful and the seemingly mediocre days of my life that God's presence doesn't depend upon you or me. The gift of God's presence is freely given twenty-four seven for as long as we live and in spite of how we choose to live. So begin this journey with every confidence that The Creator, The Everlasting, The Source of Life who is our God is absolutely and always aware of your comings and goings.

I write with gratitude to my family: Husband Mike, sons, Mike and Tim, daughters-in-law, Abby and Kim and granddaughters, Ellie, Lauren and Claire. Of all the gifts God has given me, you are the most precious.

As we begin this journey together, I offer humble thanks to my persistently patient God whose constant awareness of my comings and goings brings welcome peace to my life. It is the Everlasting Light who finds me everywhere that inspires all that I do.

Mary Penich
May 23, 2011

for Christmastime and Winter Days

Our Journey Together

Holiday vendors haven't wasted a moment displaying their Christmas wares. While I contemplated our Thanksgiving plans, others hurried to complete their Christmas shopping lists in order to take advantage of the early bird sales. I try to take a few moments to consider all that I'm grateful for in preparation for the arrival of Thanksgiving Day each year. Still, I find myself lost in the holiday frenzy before I know it. Thanksgiving comes and goes while I miss another opportunity to acknowledge the gift that this life is to me.

The pages that follow represent my effort to assist you and me in making the most of the rich and powerful days that lie ahead. It seems to me that the most efficient and effective way to do so is to remain cognizant of the One who gifts us with the moments of our lives.

We will begin our walk together on the First Sunday of Advent. During Advent, we acknowledge the Israelites' four thousand year wait for the Messiah. Throughout these four weeks, we also celebrate our own joyful anticipation of the moment more than two thousand years ago when heaven touched the earth that first Christmas Day. My Advent reflections call us to empty ourselves of the minutia that draws us away from the precious people and moments which bring meaning to our lives. When we free our hearts of these distractions, we open ourselves up to the treasures that make this life worth living.

We'll continue our journey through the Christmas Season. By Christmas Day, let's hope that you and I have found the true meaning of the birth of Jesus. Let's hope that the "feel good" moments will be a small taste of the profound gifts that came to this earth in the person of Jesus. My Christmastime reflections celebrate this Messiah who embraced humankind as a helpless child. God's presence among us as one of us gives meaning to both the seemingly insignificant and the most powerful events of our lives. More importantly, this presence underscores our value in the eyes of God.

After the holidays each year, I most regret the loss of good cheer that becomes quite obvious as cold and dismal January days replace the previous month's cheerful frenzy. Though linen sales quickly replace December's toy sales, our enthusiasm wanes as shopping and daily life once again become chores. I've included reflections for the New Year to remind us all that Christmas joy needn't be discarded with our used wrapping paper and ribbons. The angels chorused "Peace on earth" to carry us through all of our days. My reflections through January and February will hopefully keep us attuned to the peace God promised so long ago in spite of winter's raging.

The longer Sunday pieces give us something to think about for the coming week, while the shorter daily meditations offer a simple focus for each day. I draw each scripture reference from The Lectionary, Cycle B, Year ll.

The First Sunday of Advent

"Why do you let us wander, O Lord, from your ways, and harden our hearts so that we fear you not?"
Isaiah 63:17

While I consider what magic to work with the Thanksgiving leftovers that linger in the refrigerator, I wonder if I will need a bit of magic to survive the twenty-five days that remain until Christmas Day. "Survive?" I'm a bit disappointed in myself for selecting that particular word to describe my life for the next four weeks. Am I actually willing to settle for "surviving" when these days of waiting before Christmas offer so many possibilities? "Silly, Mary, very silly," I tell myself as I catch a glimpse of the lawn decorations we will debut this Christmas. Indeed, I will do much more than survive this Advent.

Mike and I are replacing the tired and worn angels that graced our lawn for a dozen Christmases with images of Charlie Brown, Linus, Lucy, Snoopy, Woodstock and their pathetic Christmas Tree. The Peanuts Gang was born just a few years before I was, and it didn't take long for me develop great affection for each one of them, especially Charlie Brown. Charlie Brown's misadventures reflect our human experience at its worst and at its best. In spite of his frailty and seemingly unending list of failures, Charlie Brown never abandons the hope with which he begins each new day. Though Lucy always drops the football before he kicks it, Charlie Brown embraces the opportunity to kick it every time. "Maybe this time," he tells himself, "I'll kick it!" Though the Pretty Little Red

Something To Think About...

Haired Girl doesn't even know Charlie Brown's name, he waits with great anticipation for her first smile. "Maybe this will be the day she notices me," he muses. Though all he can find is a thinly branched, minimally needled tree for the Christmas pageant, Charlie Brown drags it to the middle of the school stage, certain that it will be just right. Maybe this effort will finally satisfy his friends. Though most of these ventures bring about Charlie Brown's complete embarrassment, each one ends with Charlie Brown's renewed hope in the things to come. Charlie Brown remains ever faithful to his resolve to live each moment of his life and Charlie Brown remains ever hopeful that there is joy to be found in each one. Though the glare of Charlie Brown's failures tries to dissuade him, Charlie Brown never ever gives up.

It seems to me that the good Charlie Brown has much to teach us this Advent Season. Could it be that Charles Schultz referenced Isaiah when he illustrated the cycle of demise to triumph to demise to triumph that is Charlie Brown's life? Poor Isaiah speaks from his own intense suffering in today's first reading (Isaiah 63: 16-17; 64:2-7). Isaiah fumes over the Israelites continued unfaithfulness to God. He cannot tolerate their evildoing any longer. Isaiah fumes even more vigorously at the Lord God who allows the people to fall into evil repeatedly. Isaiah raises his voice to the heavens as he begs, "Why do you let us wander, O Lord, from your ways, and harden our hearts so that we fear you not?" As I read Isaiah's words, echoes of similar quandaries from my own lips swirl in my memory. How many times have I looked to our loving God and asked, "If You don't want things to be this way, why don't

You fix them?" My friend Charlie Brown may moan and wring his hands momentarily, but, in the end, he always reclaims his hope and renews his faith in the possibilities of the moment at hand. In the end, Isaiah does the same. The prophet turns his outstretched arms to God and says, "Yet, O Lord, you are our father; we are the clay and you are the potter: we are the work of your hands." Isaiah is grateful to be God's child. So am I.

Every day, you and I and our loved ones face multiple challenges. Whether it is the troubled economy or our troubled hearts, we find ourselves facing the moment without the resources we need. Whether it is the discouraging job market or our own discouragement, we find ourselves lacking in productivity. Whether it is the miles between us and our loved ones or our inability to communicate with those nearby, we find ourselves feeling very much alone. Though there is no lack of blessings in our lives, we often find ourselves blind to them.

This Advent Season invites us to wait with joyful anticipation for the coming of the Messiah. Though Isaiah had only his faith to rely upon and Charlie Brown was at the mercy of Charles Schultz's pen, we have everything we need to make the most of these days before Christmas. We know the Messiah firsthand in his word and in every good deed he did for those around him. We know the Messiah in his life and in the death he endured for each one of us. We know the Messiah in the fleeting moments of peace, joy and love that punctuate our loves. We know the Messiah in the people God has given us to love. So it is that we continue to kick that football and dream of the

Something To Think About...

Pretty Little Red Haired Girl with Charlie Brown. So it is that we look with Isaiah to God for all that we need. So it is that we live these days of waiting with great faith and great hope in the things to come

> *Dearest God, though the wonders of Creation surround me in this world and in the people I have been given to love, I lose sight of my hope. Though You promise to be with me always, I too often think I'm alone. Today, I open my heart to Your presence. Please reveal Your goodness to me.*

Monday, the First Week of Advent

*"I am not worthy to have you under my roof.
Just give an order and the boy will get better..."*
From Matthew 8:5-11

Twenty-four days remain until Christmas, surely not enough to accomplish all that I have to do. Still, my own tasks at hand loom lightly over me as I consider the trials and tribulations of those around me. I've lost far too many people that I love this past year, and I know those closest to them feel these losses more than ever today. The economy may bring better news to the wealthy just now, but plenty of people I know continue to suffer. Food pantries need more supplies. Shelters need more blankets, and curbside bell ringers clang loudly, as though their very lives depend on what I put into their little red pales.

The man who approaches Jesus to ask for his son's cure isn't used to having to beg for anything. Yet, in the face of losing his child, he sets protocol aside and begs Jesus for his son's life. The man doesn't expect Jesus to come to his home as it is not worthy of one who has power over life and death. Jesus responds to his great faith and heals the man's son just as Jesus responds to all my needs.

> *Loving God, I am worthy of your gifts only because You say that I am. Give me the generosity to share Your blessings with those who need them most. Let these kindnesses bring Christmas joy to all whom I meet this Advent.*

Something To Think About...

Tuesday, the First Week of Advent

*"The wolf shall be the guest of the lamb
and the leopard shall lie down with the kid;
the calf and the young lion shall browse together, with a little
child to lead them."*
From Isaiah 11:1-10

My granddaughter's smile draws me in before I realize what the little imp has done. My bad hair day, those extra pounds that continue to linger and my complete disappointment in myself regarding so many things mean nothing to the little one in my arms. As Claire plays with the strings of my hoodie, she looks to see that I'm watching. Then, ever so carefully, she puts the end of one string into her mouth. When I smile and ask, "Please don't eat my string," Claire eases the wet knot out of her mouth and smiles back at me. As Claire looks for something else to soothe her teething, I hug her more closely. Claire nuzzles her head into me. She nods off to sleep, and I turn my eyes upward to thank God for this precious little girl. I also offer thanks for Claire's gentle reminder that kind words and a smile are difficult to ignore.

> *During this far too busy season, Lord, please help me to remember to approach those around me with kindness and a smile. May my presence become a calming influence wherever You lead me today.*

Wednesday, the First Week of Advent

"...people came to him bringing with them the crippled, the deformed, the blind, the mute, and many others besides. They laid them at his feet and he cured them... 'My heart is moved with pity for the crowd.'"
From Matthew 15:29-37

I plan to visit Janet tomorrow. My cousin currently wages war with a brain tumor that promises to give her a very tough go of it. So far, Janet has kept her amazing attitude and her smile intact. At the same time, the tumor has kept its promise with persistent vengeance. Every good turn has been answered with one setback or another.

I marvel at my cousin's positive outlook as she's traveled this road before with her sister, who passed from cancer less than three years ago, and her brother, who passed from cancer less than a year ago. I turn to Matthew's report of the lame who now walk, the deformed who are restored and the mute who speak, and I wonder why Janet's name isn't listed among the cured. Before I voice my query to God above, the gray skies beyond my window part and the sun's golden radiance overwhelms the horizon.

> *Healing God, though my prayers for my cousin continue in full earnest, I know that your plans for her are much more wonderful than anything I ask for her. Walk with Janet as she makes her way home to you. Walk with those of us who love her. May we bring her hope to this season as we await Hope Incarnate.*

Something To Think About...

Thursday, the First Week of Advent

"Anyone who hears my words and puts them into practice is like the wise man who built his house on rock."
From Matthew 7:21, 24-27

Christmas preparations always conjure up moments of nostalgia within me. Recent losses draw me back to Christmas 1959, just five months after my dad passed away. Though I was only eight years old, I recall the efforts of those around me who made this Christmas special, perhaps in an effort to ease the sting of my dad's absence.

My older sister Rita joined our Mom in preparing a special gift for each one of us. On Christmas Eve, our parish priests asked my brother to walk his wagon down to the rectory. Raoul returned with a beautifully wrapped package for each of the six of us. After Christmas dinner, we went on to Aunt Claire's and Uncle Steve's home to celebrate with my dad's family. My aunt and uncle ushered us to their Christmas Tree for more gifts. Though all concerned knew that nothing could replace my dad, they did their best to emulate his love for us. Though I can't name the gifts I received that year, I continue to feel the love offered that has sustained me for a lifetime.

> *Generous God, You gifted me with a family who placed their love for one another above all else. As I prepare for Christmas with those you've given me to love, let my love for each one be the foundation of everything I do for them.*

Friday, the First Week of Advent

*"When his children see the work of my hands
in his midst, they shall keep my name holy..."*
From Isaiah 29:17-24

Ellie attends preschool at the church school in her neighborhood. The teacher in me is thrilled that my eldest granddaughter enjoys school so much. The teacher in me also wonders if my former students repeated verbatim the things I said to them as frequently as Ellie repeats her teacher's words. In the midst of our play, when something goes especially well, Ellie prays, "Amen! Alleluia." When I ask, "Why did you say that?" Ellie shares that her teacher says this. Ellie echoes her parents as well. When her younger sister Lauren doesn't cooperate, Ellie observes, "She's little, Grandma. I'm the big sister. I'll show her how to be good."

Ellie's learning isn't limited to the things she hears. Indeed, most of what Ellie has learned from those around her has come from their example. Her tenderness toward Lauren when she's sick and toward Baby Claire when she cries for Mommy speaks volumes regarding the lessons taught in her home.

> *Gentle God, this hectic season evokes my best and my worst at times. As I set out to prepare Christmas for those I've been given to love, keep me mindful of my attitude; for it will be the spirit in which I do these things that will be the greatest lesson and the greatest gift to those around me.*

Saturday, the First Week of Advent

*"God will be gracious to you when you cry out;
as soon as God hears, God will answer you."
From Isaiah 30:19-21, 23-26*

Years ago, one of my students shared that he was going to prove to his older brother that Santa Claus is real. Ronnie decided that he would tell no one what he wanted for Christmas except Santa. When Ronnie visited Santa during his family's annual day-after-Thanksgiving trek to the mall, he whispered into Santa's ear so his gift would remain a secret. Though I usually set aside school concerns during winter break to enjoy Christmas with my own family, that year I wondered often if Ronnie's experiment proved Santa's existence after all. Happily, Ronnie returned to school in January with a bigger-than-ever smile.

Later that year, Ronnie's mom shared that Ronnie's older brother had made her aware of Ronnie's Christmas experiment. The entire family attended to Ronnie's inadvertent hints so carefully that they discovered what he wanted for Christmas in the nick of time.

Oh God, when I see unhappiness and doubt in others, I wring my hands in despair. I wonder how I can possibly convince those around me of Your everlasting love. Sometimes, I find myself doubting You. Bless me with Ronnie's faith today and reveal Yourself in everything I do.

The Second Sunday of Advent

*"Like a shepherd he feeds his flock;
in his arms he gathers the lambs,
carrying them in his bosom..."*
From Isaiah 40:1-5, 9-11

This morning, the most wonderful pine scent greeted me as I awoke. I tiptoed into the living room to eye the beautiful Christmas-tree-to-be that waits patiently in its stand. I sat on the couch for a moment, considering this year's plan of attack for decorating. As I wondered how we will possibly be ready for Christmas, I heard my mother calling...

"Uncle Herb is here!" I grabbed my coat and ran outside to see what treasures filled his truck. Every year, my mother's uncle makes the journey north from Kankakee with a truckload of Christmas Trees for his nieces and nephews and their families. Uncle Herb lives on a huge farm with trees enough to supply the family for generations to come. Regardless of the size or fullness of Uncle Herb's trees, each year my mother fashions Uncle Herb's gift into a sparkling monument to Christmas. We're never quite sure of what to expect. One year, we chose from among a dozen eleven and twelve foot trees. Since most of our ceilings loomed about nine feet overhead, everyone had a bit of trimming to do to make the trees fit. Last year, Uncle Herb arrived with twenty-five trees that were only three or four feet tall. My mother selected five of the smallest. She stood each one in a gallon milk bottle and arranged the quintet into a beautiful arch that filled our bay window. Our home was the only one on the block that boasted an *indoor forest.* "I hope the trees are little ones this year!" I told myself. *After my mother welcomed Uncle Herb with a hug, she called us to the truck to check this year's inventory. The wonderful scent of pine distracted me from the task of selecting a tree. How I love the scent of pine...*

The clock on the piano ticked just loudly enough to steal me away from my memories. The vivid images that warmed my heart so can't possibly be fifty years old! Throughout my childhood, the Christmas Season provided me the closest experience to heaven that we humans can enjoy during our tenure in this life. This Second Sunday of Advent, I look to the days to come with watchful eyes and an unsteady heart. The simple memories of my childhood Christmases touch me deeply. Yet, somehow, I find myself at a loss as I attempt to fashion this Advent and Christmas into equally powerful experiences for my own family. Perhaps, I must look beyond my childhood memories and beyond my own frailty to God's promise of the things to come.

The God of Isaiah and Peter, Mark and John the Baptist engages in every attempt to make this life a memory that will guide us on to the next. The scriptures report event after event through which God nurtures a strong relationship with humankind. No matter how far from God we wander, God calls out to us with open arms with the promise to remain present to us in our lives. Today's readings give each of us good reason to rejoice over our God's effort. Perhaps God's generous investment will inspire us to return this gesture with our own investment in our relationships with God, particularly during this advent of Christmas.

In Isaiah 40:1-5; 9-11, the prophet heralds the onset of new times for his people. Isaiah tells us that the Lord's passionate love for us has not run out. The Lord God is the shepherd who "...feeds his flock; in his arms he gathers the lambs, carrying them in his bosom." We are the lambs drawn unto our Shepherd today. If we will, we can rest comfortably in God's warm embrace, wondering at the mystery of a love so great. In 2 Peter 3:8-14, Peter echoes Isaiah's call to look to the Lord for all that we need. For it is in the Lord God, who is revealed in the person of Jesus, that we find true peace. In Mark 1:1-8, the evangelist uses Isaiah's words to underscore the importance of Jesus' coming. Mark calls our attention to the announcement by John the Baptist that the presence of God is among us. Mark begins his gospel with this message that must not be missed. Indeed, God is here. Just as I savor the Christmas memories of my childhood, we savor the scriptures, the record book of the childhood of God's People.

Uncle Herb's love for his nieces and nephews and my mom's love for me, my brother and sisters are part and parcel of who I am. In the same way, Divine love defines you and me as God's beloved children. This Advent provides us a not-to-be-missed opportunity to celebrate this love as we prepare for the coming of Jesus. We can begin by looking to the joyful memories of Christmases past, by making the most of the possibilities of Christmas present, while embracing the promise of eternal life in

Something To Think About...

Christmas to come.

> *Dearest God, though the wonders of Creation surround me in this world and in the people I have been given to love, I sometimes lose sight of You. Though You promise to be with me always, I too often attempt to face the challenges of this life alone. Today, I welcome Your presence. Please walk with me this Advent as I prepare to celebrate Christmas.*

Monday, the Second Week of Advent

*"Say to those whose hearts are frightened:
Be strong, fear not!
...They will meet with joy and gladness,
sorrow and mourning will flee."
From Isaiah 35:1-10*

Most of my students counted the days to Christmas vacation with great relish. Some years, one or two dreaded this departure from their daily routines. These children lived in dire poverty. School lunches were the best of their meals and our simple class parties were the best of their Christmases. Too often, the lack of material treasures in their lives paled in the shadow of the lack of love and security. The adults around them, heavily burdened with their own troubles, never saw the hurt and the hopelessness growing in their children's eyes.

As Christmas draws near, I can't help thinking about these special children who appreciated the little gifts I hid in their backpacks almost as much as they appreciated my attention throughout the day at school. Though I will be bombarded with requests to assist the needy over the days to come and though I don't have the resources to alleviate all of the poverty in this world, I will do something.

God of love, help me to bring gladness and joy to those in need. Let them find Your love in my smile and Your hope in what I am able to share.

Tuesday, the Second Week of Advent

*"Comfort, give comfort to my people,
says your God."
From Isaiah 40:1-11*

Janet's day wasn't going well. Though she'd endured occupational therapy that morning, she refused to participate in physical therapy that afternoon. Janet had developed sensitivity in her skin, so much so that a gentle touch brought great pain. Her back and legs hurt, too. Janet's only relief came with sleep. When I arrived, Janet was sleeping while her fiancé rested at her bedside. Bob gave me an update on Janet's condition and then half-jokingly added that the food at this rehabilitation facility left much to be desired. Bob noted that one of the few meals Janet had enjoyed was some broccoli cheese soup from a nearby restaurant. Janet woke a while later, just in time for dinner. When the prospect of another institutional meal threatened, Janet returned to her nap. I offered to make a "soup run" for Janet. Bob tried not to smile too broadly as he responded, "If you don't mind..." Twenty minutes later, Janet happily savored every drop of that soup! Afterward, she settled into a most content nap.

Comforting God, You've soothed Janet's pain through the smallest kindnesses of those who love her. Today, help me to comfort those who need to feel Your Presence with a "soup run" or whatever else I can do to help.

Wednesday, the Second Week of Advent
"Come to me, all you who are weary and find life burdensome, and I will give you rest..."
From Matthew 11:28-30

Presentation Church stood one block west and around the corner from our two-flat on Polk Street. This gray stone edifice proved to be the most significant landmark in my life. My parents married there. My siblings and I were baptized there. We celebrated my uncle's and grandfather's funerals there. The morning my dad passed away, my mom woke me to share this devastating news. Without hesitation, I dressed and ran down the street to church. When our parish priest saw me there alone, he knew that the inevitable had occurred. After offering me his shoulder to cry on, he sat me in the pew next to him —a humble substitute for my Dad. Father knelt to finish his prayers, and I looked through my tear-filled eyes at this church which had become a second home to me. When I peered at the ceiling, I read the golden inscription over the altar: "Come to me all you who labor and are burdened and I will give you rest." No wonder my dad had gone to heaven. God was waiting there to make him better.

Dearest Lord, Your home became my home because Jesus revealed your welcoming love to me in everything he said and did. I will prepare for Christmas Day by bringing Jesus' message of welcome to everyone I meet along the way.

Something To Think About...

Thursday, the Second Week of Advent

*"Let all your works give you thanks, O Lord,
and let your faithful ones bless you."
From Psalm 145*

Ellie and Lauren happily endure the wait for Christmas by attending to their Advent Calendars. One calendar celebrates Christmas Joy to come. Each day, the girls take turns placing a little stuffed animal or person onto the calendar's Nativity scene that hangs in their kitchen. On December 25, Baby Jesus will complete the scene. Two other calendars rest on the kitchen counter. Every day, Ellie opens one door on her calendar and Lauren opens one door on hers. Behind each numbered door rests a tiny piece of chocolate. These usually forbidden treats give my little granddaughters a small taste of the joyful anticipation that is meant to characterize our Advent observances.

As Ellie and Lauren savor those tiny bits of chocolate, I consider how I might savor this joyful time of waiting.

> *God of Isaiah, Abraham and Moses, how blessed I am to know the promises of that first Christmas. Please help me to anticipate this Christmas joyfully by celebrating Your presence among us every moment of every day.*

Friday, the Second Week of Advent

*"They are like children squatting in
the town square, calling to their playmates,
'We piped you a tune but you did not dance.
We sang you a dirge but you did not wail.'"
From Matthew 11:16-19*

My colleague threw up her hands in disgust. "I told them not to do that. I told them precisely what to do and when to do it. They had to have it their own way and now we're in a mess." As my friend lamented what her students had done regarding "their" class Christmas Pageant, I couldn't help smiling to myself. In a calmer moment, my friend would have been the first to admit that she likes things to go her own way -period. I dared not bring this up as her students' plans for costumes, scenery and refreshments had created a seemingly impossible-to-meet time-line for their class production. Instead, I offered to help. In the end, the kids did a wonderful job surprising their teacher with their creativity, their work ethic and a wonderful play. Though my friend grew some additional gray hair in the process, she also cultivated a deep respect for this special class who surprised her in many more amazing ways before June.

Patient God, more often than not, I want to do things my way. More often than not, I leave others out as I try to do everything myself. This Advent, please open my ears to the numerous offers to help around me and open my heart to accept them.

Something To Think About...

Saturday, the Second Week of Advent
*"Take care of this vine,
and protect what your right hand has planted.'"
From Psalm 80*

We are two weeks into Advent, and I find myself assessing my progress today. While I've managed to take care of most of my Christmas shopping, I've had a bit of trouble maintaining an attitude of joyful anticipation. I'm certainly anticipating Christmas. It is the "joyful" part that has been difficult.

My own family is generously blessed, and I express my gratitude to the Lord God daily —sometimes several times a day. Still, others for whom I care deeply suffer greatly. I feel helpless as there isn't much that I can do for them just now. So it is that I pray that peace will come their way. When nothing seems to change, I become impatient and begin ordering the Almighty to take care of things. "I wouldn't talk to You this way," I say, "if You'd fix this!" It is usually after such a conversation that I run into these loved ones. They inadvertently share that though all is not well, God is with them and they are at peace. It is then that I kneel before God to apologize. Afterward, I also pray that I'll develop some patience by Christmas.

Patient God, as I ready myself for Christmas, I know You ready each of us for our journey home to You. Forgive me for questioning Your wisdom and Your love.

The Third Sunday of Advent

*"I am a voice in the desert crying out:
Make straight the way of the Lord."
From John 1:6-8, 19-28*

My husband and I are grateful that we're able to see our three granddaughters often. When we visit, Little Claire rests in Grandpa Mike's arms while her older sisters move about the family room playing, dancing and talking. As I watch her, I realize Little Claire is actually just as busy as her sisters are. Claire is simply busy in a different way. While Ellie's and Lauren's activity is quite obvious, Claire's is so subtle that one not watching her carefully will miss it. Claire's activity is in her eyes. She looks with great interest at Grandpa's face. When he smiles, she tries to do the same. When he talks, Claire does her best to make audible sounds that only she can interpret. Most of the time, Claire seems to be looking into Grandpa's eyes. When he blinks, she responds. When he opens his eyes very wide, Claire seems to try to do the same. When Grandpa looks away from her, Claire wiggles or makes a sound to draw his eyes back to her. Claire seems most content looking into the eyes of the one who holds her, especially if this is Mommy. It is during these moments of complete peace and serenity that Claire is most likely to fall asleep.

Though Ellie is now four years old and Lauren is three, they haven't forgotten the effectiveness of the eyes of those around them. They've been aware of the power of eye contact for quite some time.

About a year and a half ago, we were having dinner

with our children and grandchildren when Ellie decided that she'd had enough to eat. Rather than interrupting our chatter with her usual proclamation, "All done!" Ellie swept her arm across her plate and propelled her leftovers across the table and onto the floor. Our son, Mike, responded immediately. He took Ellie's hands into his own and said, "Ellie, look at me. Look at Daddy. We don't throw our food. Look at Daddy, Ellie..." and so it went. Ellie kept her head turned completely away from her father because she wanted no part of a conversation regarding her behavior. Indeed, she avoided eye contact with Mommy, Grandpa, Uncle Tim, Aunt Kim and me until Daddy was willing to drop the subject. Good Daddy that he is, my son simply announced that Ellie was finished as he removed Ellie's plate from her reach. One last time, he addressed the subject. "We don't throw our food, Ellie. All you have to do is say 'All done.'" With absolute faith in Daddy's willingness to forgive her, Ellie looked him in the eye and said, "All done." Ellie kept her eyes locked in his as Daddy said, "That's good, Ellie. Good girl." The little imp looked around the table, making eye contact with each member of the adoring family who reveled in her new-found redemption.

It seems to me that Ellie touched on the heart of John the Baptizer's message that day. John's gospel tells us that John the Baptizer has drawn the attention of many, including the temple hierarchy. The people in Jerusalem sent priests, Levites and even Pharisees to question John about his identity. "Who are you?" Each one presses John, asking if he is the Prophet or Elijah or the Christ. Each time, John replies, "I am not." Finally, John goes on to tell all who will listen, "I am the voice of one crying out in the desert, 'Make straight the way of the Lord.' ...there is one among you whom you do not recognize, the one who is coming after me, whose sandal strap I am not worthy to untie." John seems to say, "Open your eyes. God is with you!" Sadly, the temple officials fail to look John the Baptizer in the eye as he speaks and they fail to take his message into their hearts. So it is that they fail to recognize that John is the emissary of He who is to come. God is among the people, but because they fail to look carefully at what they see, they miss the One for whom they've waited centuries. Ellie, Lauren and Claire clearly understand the importance of looking carefully at who is important to them. Unlike the contemporaries of John the Baptizer, my granddaughters use their eyes to peer into the heart of what matters most.

Not many days remain until Christmas. Some of us fret over "to do" lists that are far too long. Some of us fret over Christmas Wish Lists that the economy simply will not allow us to fulfill. Others of us fret over the impending heartbreak of Christmas without our loved ones. Still others fret over the sadness of spending Christmas alone. In the midst of our worry, it is most imperative that each of us listens to the voice that cries out in the desert and looks into the eyes of the One who takes our hands into his own. "Look at me. Look at Daddy," He says. "If only you keep your eyes locked in Mine, all will be well. If only you keep your eyes locked in Mine, you will see the peace and serenity that await you. Just a few days remain until Christmas. If only you keep your eyes locked in Mine, there will be time for everything that matters."

Something To Think About...

Dear and Loving God, when I allow myself quiet moments with You, the eyes of my heart see into Your loving eyes. Today and for the days that remain this Advent, I promise to spend ten minutes alone with You, eye to eye and heart to heart.

Monday, the Third Week of Advent
*"On what authority are you doing these things.
Who has given you this power?"
From Matthew 21:23-27*

When I taught, I prided myself in remaining calm in the face of misbehavior. My students' apparently agreed, as their subsequent compliance proved me right. Still, I admit to allowing my anger to get the best of me the morning I heard that a former student had died. Though he had a good and kind heart, Lee had also been taken in by the allure of the streets more than once. This time, he drove a van that his friends had loaded with stolen bicycles from a nearby suburb. A police chase resulted in the accident that took Lee's life. In the wake of this news, a fifth grade boy began bragging that he was in the van during that chase and that he flew out the door and ran away when the van tipped over on its side. Before he could finish his yarn, I called him over. "Who do you think you are?" I wailed. "Lee died last night and you were nowhere near that van. Don't you dare try to make yourself look cool on the life of my friend!" The target of my ire slinked back to his classroom without uttering another word.

> *Dear God, when those I love and those I should love more lose battles with the challenges of this life, I sometimes question who any of us are. Yet, You make our identities as your beloved children quite clear. Help me to embrace my place in Your Family this Christmas and always.*

Something To Think About...

Tuesday, the Third Week of Advent

*"I will leave as a remnant in your midst
a people humble and lowly,
Who shall take refuge in the name of the Lord."
From Zephaniah 3:1-2, 9-13*

Thank God for the buoys among us who keep us on the right path and raise us up when we threaten to sink into the depths of despair! I'm so grateful for what these inspirational souls do for me. In return, I try to do the same for those around me by writing. This effort began nineteen years ago when Father Farrell Kane worked on compiling our first parish bulletin. Because I was a teacher, Father felt certain that I could come up with "something inspirational" to fill up this first edition. Apparently, our kindhearted parishioners agreed as I've been doing so ever since.

The best part of all of this is that I'm committed to several hours of reflection and "God time" in order to provide an article for that bulletin each week. I've found that I wander aimlessly much less often than I used to because of this focus.

> *You know, God, that though they don't write for me every week, I'm blessed with many wonderful people who inspire me with their goodness day after day. As we prepare for Christmas together, please remind these and all of Your children of the many ways in which they provide unique inspiration to me and to one another.*

Wednesday, the Third Week of Advent

*"Summoning two of his disciples,
John sent them to ask the Lord,
'Are you He who is to come
or are we to expect someone else?'"
From Luke 7:18-23*

Sometimes, the daily news is too much for any of us to endure. Troops overseas, the economy, cuts in healthcare and education and the inability for our legislators to agree on much of anything threaten to rend our last threads of hope. Still, we continue our Christmas preparations. My husband the deacon works on his homily. I prepare an article for the early Christmas bulletin deadline. I breathe deeply every time I pass our fresh Christmas Tree. I've wrapped most of the gifts and check my stocking stuffer list once again. Our budget already includes something special for those who need a little boost just now, and our parish giving campaign characteristically reached beyond all of our expectations.

We hold onto our hope in difficult times because Jesus answered John the Baptist's question with proof of better things to come: "The blind recover their sight, cripples walk, lepers are cured, the deaf hear, dead men are raised to life and the poor have the good news preached to them."

> *Dear God, we hold onto Your gift of hope. It came to us in the Person of Jesus two millennia ago. It comes again and again, every moment of our lives, in Your Presence among us.*

Something To Think About...

Thursday, the Third Week of Advent

*"I assure you, there is no man
born of woman greater than John.
Yet the least born into the kingdom of God
is greater than he."
From Luke 7:24-30*

As Christmas approaches, memories of Christmas Past fill me up. Year after year, our large family gathered to celebrate this favorite of all holidays. This year, I'm struck hard by the number of family members I've lost. My mom had seven siblings and all have joined her in the hereafter. My dad was one of twelve and only two of his siblings remain with us. I lost my brother Raoul and several of my cousins decades earlier than my family ever expected. When we gathered for the wakes and funerals of each of these loved ones, our conversations included not only our favorite reminiscing, but also our projections regarding their current activities at home with God.

When Jesus acknowledged the greatness of anyone who makes it home to God, he offered us more hope than we could ever have imagined and more reason to celebrate than we would otherwise have known possible.

> *Eternal God, it is with great joy that I look forward to celebrating the birth of Jesus. His coming revealed Your unconditional love and Your amazing plans for each one of us. So it is that I also look forward to life with You and with all of my loved ones who've made it home.*

Friday, the Third Week of Advent

*"For my house shall be called
a house of prayer for all peoples."
From Isaiah 56:1-3, 6-8*

During a recent parish meeting, we discussed our Christmas Mass schedule and how to accommodate the droves of people who'll attend each service. Such discussions often include a comment about the "Christmas and Easter Birds" whose only appearances for worship occur on these two holy days. Still, we make every effort to seat as many people as possible as comfortably as possible. All concerned work extremely hard preparing our beautifully adorned church, amazing music and engaging liturgy. Everyone from our youngest parish children to our devoted seniors is involved. Our hope is that we'll help all those who join us to feel welcome as they gather to worship together. After all, it's Christmas!

> *Loving God, You open Your house to all who come to Your door. While some of us feel free to knock often, there are others who stay away. Please reveal Yourself in our efforts as we prepare for Christmas so that all of Your children realize that they are welcome to Your home any time.*

Something To Think About...

Saturday, the Third Week of Advent
"A family record of Jesus Christ..."
From Matthew 1:1-17

Every year, I update my Christmas Card address file. As time passes, I've found that this task takes longer and longer because my stockpile of memories continues to grow. Usually, I smile my way through this work in response to the images of loved ones that dance in my head. This year, my encounter with my list of family members and friends is bittersweet. A renewed sense of loss emerges each time I come to the name of someone who has passed away since last Christmas. I tell myself that if I truly believe, I must know that these loved ones are attending Jesus' birthday celebration in person this year. I giggle at a mental picture of that amazing birthday cake with all of those candles as I get back to work.

Caring God, now I understand why Matthew begins his gospel with a listing of Jesus' family tree members all the way back to Abraham. Before he begins sharing the teachings of Jesus, Matthew wishes to make it crystal clear that Jesus fully embraced our humanity. Jesus teaches from the heart and soul of a family member and friend who fully understands our joys and our sorrows. Thank you, Jesus, for coming as one of us!

The Fourth Sunday of Advent

"Rejoice, O highly favored daughter! The Lord is with you. Blessed are you among women."
From Luke 1:26-38

I remember as though it was yesterday... The UPS driver who frequents the neighborhood interrupted our dinner. When I went to the door, this consistently polite gentleman greeted me with a peculiar smile. He handed me a very small, flat package which I eagerly accepted. I wondered if Mr. UPS smiled because of the package's size or because he somehow knew that I'd been waiting eagerly for this particular delivery. I told him as much as I returned his smile and offered my thanks.

On my way back to the kitchen table, I quickly opened the little cardboard envelope. "It's my proof!" I announced as I stared at the little yellow book in my hands. The joy I felt at that moment is indescribable. I can tell you that it filled me up from head to toe, front to back, inside and outside. I'd written this little book years ago. My nephew, Ralph, had drawn the illustrations for me. Though I had a classroom-size copy made which I read to my students many times over the years, I'd never gotten around to having the book published. Finally seeing this work in print absolutely overwhelmed me.

When my husband put down his fork to peruse the book, I looked over his shoulder. As Mike thumbed through the pages, I realized that there were errors in the copy. "Oh brother!" I remarked. "They printed the wrong file." I set the book aside while we finished dinner. As we ate, I found myself staring at the cover again and again, unable to contain my smile. Though there was work to be done to correct the flaws, I treasured this tiny volume. A week later, when the corrected proof arrived, I happily inspected the shiny yellow cover. I checked every page and finally approved the copy for print. Afterward, I placed the new proof on my desk under the original. After all, it was the original proof that brought me that amazing joy, and I was reluctant to file it away.

This Fourth Sunday of Advent, I find that my little yellow book adventure hints at God's work among us these days of Advent and always. Do you remember the Creation Story? God's love is so great that it overflowed into a universe filled with awesome beauty and wonder. Still, this material expanse wasn't enough. God went on to create creatures great and small to roam this earth. Though the microbes and insects, fish and whales, cows, dinosaurs and dogs enhanced life on this planet, love impelled God to create souls capable of receiving the love that began it all. If those souls responded in kind, they would share God's love with one another. God rejoiced in the possibilities that lay ahead. In Genesis 1:31 we read, "God saw all that he had made, and it was very good." If I so passionately treasure my flawed little book, what must God feel about us —the wondrous work of God's hands?

My little yellow book adventure hints at more. Do you remember what occurred after Creation? Though we and the world around us are the fruit of God's love, from the very beginning humankind managed to distort that love at every turn. Adam and Eve ate of the single forbidden tree in the garden. Their son Cain killed his brother Abel out of jealousy. The scriptures go on to tell us that as God's children multiplied, so did our sinfulness. The good news is that God responded to every new generation of transgressions with opportunities to begin anew once again. God considered all of creation –including us– to be very good at the beginning of time, and God's opinion remains intact today. If I cannot bring myself to discard the flawed version of my little book, can I actually believe that God would discard one of us any more easily?

Only a few days of Advent remain, and there is much for all of us to do before Christmas Day. In spite of the length of your errand list, may I ask you to add just one more item? At the very top of your list, write GOD, G-O-D. Every time you look at the list, while you're waiting in line, driving to the next store or pumping another tank of gas, think of the One who's at the top of your list because you are at the top of God's list. Regardless of what does and doesn't get accomplished this week, God will look upon you with pride. Whether you're shopping for a family member or someone in need, God will look upon you with appreciation. If you manage the holidays well because your life is good or simply because you've set aside your own worries for the moment, God will look upon you with admiration. Most important of all, remember that even if you forget the One at the top of your list, God will look upon you with great love –always, in all ways.

We will make the best of these last days of Advent because we are blessed among men and women, young and old, healthy and infirmed. We give God joy from head

Something To Think About...

to toe, front to back, inside and outside. Because God's affection overflows into our hearts, this love will overflow from us onto those we've been given to love! What more can we ask for?

> *Dearest God, thank You for Your many reminders that we are, indeed, highly favored. Be with each one of us as we complete our Christmas preparations. Transform everything we do for those we've been given to love into a reminder of their "highly favored" status with You!*

Monday, the Fourth Week of Advent

*"How am I to know this?
I am an old man; my wife is advanced in age...."
From Luke 1:5-25*

Aunt Lucille lost my Uncle Leonard when he was only thirty-six years old. Brave woman that she was, she walked head-on into her new life with her three young children in tow. Though many suitors attempted to woo her into marriage, Aunt Lucille kept them at arm's length until her children were adults and on their own. It was then my soon-to-be uncle came along. Bill swept Aunt Lucille off her feet and down the aisle, much to all of our joy. Not long afterward, Lucille experienced some odd symptoms that prompted her to see the doctor. When her amazed physician announced that Aunt Lucille was pregnant –at age forty-seven!- my poor aunt panicked. How would she tell Bill? Though I'm uncertain of the words she chose, I do know that Bill responded with absolute ecstasy. After all, Bill was only fifty-seven!

O God of Wisdom, Your timing is indeed impeccable. As Christmas draws near and the unexpected threatens to thwart my efforts, keep me mindful that Your plans will be fulfilled -no matter what!

Tuesday, the Fourth Week of Advent

*"Mary said, 'I am the maidservant of the Lord.
Let it be done to me as you say.'"
From Luke 1:26-38*

Our Christmas Tree reigns supreme over the living room. Though it is the tree's fragrance that invariably beckons me in to appreciate its splendor, it is the village at its feet that keeps my attention. Every year, my husband lies on the floor under our tree for hours to fashion his current vision of Bethlehem. Though Mike's placement of the houses and trees, cars, figures and skating pond vary from year to year, they always sit in humble deference to the crèche.

When the hustle and hassle of these last days of Advent threaten my Christmas Spirit, I come to the place where Mary's "yes" to the Angel Gabriel came to fruition. As I gaze at Mary and her baby, I consider the difficulties that turned this poor teenager's world upside-down. I realize the insignificance of my own little troubles in the grand scheme of things and I thank God for this sometimes crazy life.

> *Generous God, today I will honor the memory of Jesus' mother with my patience and perseverance, my gratitude and my graciousness. Give me the generosity of spirit to say "yes" with Mary's determination to all that You ask of me.*

Wednesday, the Fourth Week of Advent

"O my dove in the clefts of the rock, in the secret recesses of the cliff, let me see you, let me hear your voice, for your voice is sweet and lovely."
From the Song of Solomon 2:8-14

My husband serves as a deacon at our church and happily witnesses several weddings each year. Mike provides marriage preparation and assists couples in planning their wedding ceremonies. Mike has found many couples to be amazingly adept at selecting scripture readings. This important day means everything to them and the readings they choose reflect this.

Passages from the Song of Solomon cited above are common selections. The truth is that our dear friend, Scott, read one such selection at our wedding almost four decades ago. Mike and I were taken in by the painful longing this lover expresses for his beloved. What we didn't fully appreciate is that the lover who speaks so passionately is the God of Israel who seeks desperately to be reunited with the Jewish People. God's longing persisted for centuries, as evidenced in the gift of Jesus. On that first Christmas, God finally expressed this unrequited love face-to-face and heart-to-heart in the gentle cooing of a newborn baby.

Loving God, thank You for the gift of Jesus. Jesus reminds us in everything he said and did that You continue to search high and low for us. Today, busy as I am, I'll slow down so You can catch me!

Something To Think About...

Thursday, the Fourth Week of Advent

*"My soul magnifies the Lord
and my spirit rejoices in God my savior,
for God has looked down upon this servant in her lowliness;
all ages to come shall call me blessed."
From Luke 1:46-56*

Since childhood, the Magnificat has been a favorite hymn of mine. When I was in the elementary school choir at Presentation Parish, we frequently sang Mary's prayer in Latin. I took Mary's words to heart. I imagined her full of joy, unable to contain her love for God's Child whom she carried within her. In my childhood innocence, I pictured a Hallmark Card Mary. Full of peace, she needed only to bow her head in prayer and wait for her baby's birth. "God will take care of everything!" I imagined her saying.

Life has taught me that things weren't quite as easy for Mary as my childhood musings suggest. In reality, Mary embarked upon a treacherous journey when she became pregnant. She succeeded only because she used all of her might to embrace the God who called her. Though her worldly lot would be uncomfortable at best, Mary trusted from beginning to end in God's faithfulness to her.

God of Mary, You are faithful to me as well. I look forward to our celebration this Christmas Day when I will taste a morsel of Mary's joy and Your unshakable love for me.

Friday, the Fourth Week of Advent
*"What will this child be?
Was not the hand of the Lord upon him?"
From Luke 1:57-66*

My little family has been on my mind all week. Every time I walk past the gifts I've wrapped for them I imagine their reactions. My granddaughters, Ellie and Lauren, have given up their fascination with gift wrap and turned their attention to the gifts inside. One-year-old Claire still relishes the opportunity to pull bows and rip paper to her heart's content. Daughter's-in-law Abby and Kim will love their gifts because they provide precise wish lists that my husband and I can easily (and happily) follow. Our sons, Mike and Tim, are another story. Old as they are, they've studied and shaken the gifts left in sight over the past few weeks. I've purposely disguised almost everything my husband and I are giving them to throw them off.

The truth is that my little family has been on my mind all week —not their gifts, but each one of them. Though none of us is perfect, the hand of the Lord has truly blessed us all and I am most grateful.

> *I thank you with all of my heart, Dearest God, for the family and friends you have given me to love. Help me and all of these precious people to share Your love wherever we find ourselves.*

Christmas Eve

"Now this is how the birth of Jesus Christ came about.
When his mother Mary was engaged to Joseph,
but before they lived together,
she was found with child..."
From Matthew 1:1-25

If your day is going like mine, you're extremely busy and a little stressed. You're finding that your meticulous planning has been helpful, but hasn't prevented last minute catastrophes of every magnitude. None of this is anyone's fault. Others could have been a little more organized, still... Christmas Eve is a busy, crazy day.

Take a little walk with me to find the crèche in your home. Whether it's situated in a lovely scene under your Christmas Tree, rests on a table or takes the form of a beautiful Christmas Card, look at the mother gazing at her newborn son. This poor child –just a teen herself- had to share the worst news with her parents. She'd become pregnant and couldn't even produce the Father for them. Still, look at her. Mary wouldn't trade places with anyone else in the world. As crazy as today and tomorrow will be, neither would you or I.

> *Generous God, thank You for bringing joy to the moments of our lives. Glory to You in the highest and peace on earth to all people of good will!*

Christmas Day

"While they were there, the days of her confinement were completed. She gave birth to her first-born son and wrapped him in swaddling clothes and laid him in a manger."
From Luke 2:1-14

Mary draws her son close to herself to kiss his forehead. His eyes open just long enough to reveal the depth of their color. The newborn sleeps again, content to nestle in his mother's arms. The rhythm of her heartbeat eases the child into deep slumber. A grateful Mary leans back against the cold wall as she embraces Jesus. Her heart feels as though it will burst within her, for she loves her son more than it is possible to love...

One wonders what the Child's Father is thinking in the distance... "Mary is the most perfect of my children, untouched by the sinfulness of the rest. Yet, in spite of their foolishness, I love them all. I cannot resist them, for everything I have made is good, and they are my greatest work. When I willed their world into being, I envisioned a kingdom. This realm would not be ruled by a monarch. It would be inspired by love. I breathed life into my first children, that they might evolve into lovers as insatiable as I. Though I gave them a pleasing appearance, I blessed them far more with pleasing spirits. In my image and likeness, I set them out to be fruitful. I set them out to experience the joy that their lives are meant to be.

"When they used their gifts as the means to walk away from me, I lingered in their shadows. I knew too well the pain and sorrow that lurked on the path ahead. How *could I allow them to embark alone upon the journey they had chosen? When the faithful among them opened their hearts to me, I revealed myself to them. Noah, Abraham and Sarah, Isaac, Moses and Aaron, Isaiah and David began to understand. When they sinned with the rest of my children, they persisted in turning back to me to begin again. How they worked to honor the Covenant and to align their hearts with my own!*

"It was not enough, I know. Their feeble sensibilities did not comprehend the depth of my love for them. So I pursue them further in the person of my son. Dearest Mary, your innocent devotion honors me. As I watch you cradle my son, I long to draw you and each of your sisters and brothers to myself. Just as your love and tenderness nurture him, this child will nurture the world with my tenderness and love. If only each one of them could feel my embrace as Jesus feels your embrace this holy night. If only they will learn to embrace one another..."

I cannot pretend to know what God was thinking the night of Jesus' birth. I can, however, turn to Jesus' life to gain some sense of the passion with which God loves us. Jesus was born among the poor, that every one of us might feel welcome in his company. Jesus honored his father and mother, that we might find honor as parents. Jesus learned a trade and worked to care for his family, that we might find satisfaction in our labor. Jesus left everything to embrace his calling, that we might find the courage to follow our hearts as well. Jesus illustrated our God's capacity to love through the story of the Prodigal

Son and in his own actions. Jesus was incapable of walking away from a soul who needed him. Jesus healed each one of obvious physical afflictions and the festering sores that disfigured his or her heart. Jesus wept at the death of his friend Lazarus, and he weeps with us over our losses. Jesus stepped into our shoes to show us how to walk graciously through this life. Jesus embraced all of humanity with God's loving hands, reminiscent of his first embrace in the arms of Mary.

This Christmas, we join our Loving God in celebrating Mary's generosity in bearing and nurturing Jesus. Mary's life changed forever the night of Jesus' birth and so changed the life of this world. The child Jesus felt love for the first time in the arms of his mother. In turn, Jesus taught this lesson of love in all that he said and did. Jesus could not contain his love for those around him any more than Mary could contain the love she felt for Jesus. This Christmas, we are invited to do the same for ourselves and for those we have been given to love. We are invited to open our hearts as Mary did and to allow God's Son to change our lives forever. In doing so, we discover the reality of Christmas: True peace and true joy come in acknowledging God's love for us, in accepting that love and in sharing that love with one another.

Merry Christmas, O God! Merry Christmas, Mary and Joseph! Happy Birthday, Jesus! Thank you for transforming this world with God's love!

Something To Think About...

The Feast of St. Stephen - December 26

"As Stephen was being stoned, he could be heard praying, 'Lord Jesus, receive my spirit.'"
From Acts of the Apostles 6:8-10; 7:54-59

The day after Christmas is a gift in itself. Though most of our Christmas observances don't go as planned, they "go" nonetheless. Our meals are often less than perfect and a few of our gifts might have been better off left at the store, yet we shared them. An attitude or two could have been adjusted a bit more positively. Still, together we created the memories that we savor today.

In spite of the imperfections of life on this earth, we celebrate the life of the One who offered heaven to us from the hands of a baby. Like good Saint Stephen, when we hung him on a cross to die, Jesus turned to God above to hand over his spirit –but not before he forgave us for rejecting the gift of himself.

> *God of Wisdom, who else could have known that becoming one of us was the best way to reveal Yourself to us? Today, I give thanks for the gift of Jesus who has truly changed my life –for the better!*

The Feast of St. John - December 27

"...what we have seen and heard we proclaim now to you."
From John 1:1-4

When I was a little girl, I asked my dad if he minded that his birthday fell two days after Christmas. He replied that this was okay because he felt as though Christmas was a very good day that led into his own very, very good day. My grandparents had little money, which leads me to believe that my dad didn't receive many gifts on either day. Still, he shared his memories with a smile big enough to convince this daughter that his childhood Christmases and birthdays were just fine.

> *Dear Jesus, thank you for choosing to live humbly among us and for teaching us to find joy in whatever our circumstances may be. More importantly, thank you for my dad who passed your teaching on to me with great competence and great love.*

Something To Think About...

The Feast of the Holy Innocents
December 28

*"The angel of the Lord appeared to Joseph in a dream and said,
'Rise, take the child and his mother,
flee to Egypt and stay there until I tell you.'"
From Matthew 2:13-18*

My family will gather again in a few days to continue our Christmastime festivities with a New Year's Day reunion. For generations before I arrived, my dad's Canadian family preserved this tradition which includes a blessing. Each year, we gather before our eldest family member to request this blessing. This one in turn asks God to provide for each one of us during the coming year.

My earliest memories include the sense of peace I felt as we knelt together in prayer. Afterward, I felt protected somehow, regardless of what life had in store for the next three hundred and sixty-five days. Perhaps this is the reason I felt the need to protect my younger sisters when our dad passed away. Perhaps this is the reason I was always careful to help my own sons to feel safe. Perhaps this is the reason I hold my granddaughters so close these days...

> *Gentle Jesus, your parents had a terrible time early on in your life. How frightening it must have been for them to witness such hatred toward a tiny baby. Today, I thank you for revealing God's unconditional love and care for me. I promise to pass it on to those I've been given to love.*

The Fifth Day of Christmas
December 29

*"Lord, now let your servant go in peace;
your word has been fulfilled: my own eyes have seen the
salvation which you prepared."
From Luke 2:22-35*

The Christmas Season summons the best of memories. Still, I can't escape the melancholy that comes with thoughts of those who've passed on to eternal life. My family is large, and it seems that with each passing year comes another loss. This past year, there were three.

As I consider the glistening snow outside of my window, I recall the glistening eyes of those who've gone home to God. As a child, my dad assured me that our family members who passed on found new health and great happiness in heaven. Over the years, I've come to recognize something in the eyes of those preparing to move on that confirms my dad's assertion. Two days before my mom passed on, I asked her if she was afraid. "Oh no, Mary. It's beautiful over there!" was her reply. Perhaps, Like Simeon, Mom's own eyes had seen.

> *Jesus, you surprise us often with glimpses of heaven in the goodness that we find around us. Today, I am most grateful for the amazing things that you reveal to our loved ones as they prepare for their journeys home to you.*

The Sixth Day of Christmas
December 30

"The child grew in size and strength, filled with wisdom, and the grace of God was upon him."
From Luke 2:36-40

As the New Year approaches, my thoughts turn to my hopes and dreams, worries and fears for 2012. I've been blessed with an inner calm that I really can't explain. Still, I fret with the best of them on occasion, especially when a loved one faces peril that I can do nothing about. When this occurs, I head outdoors to walk.

My walks aren't a retreat from my troubles. Indeed, they're just the opposite. It is while I'm embraced by a soft summer breeze or a gust of winter cold that I feel most like the child of whom Luke wrote so long ago. Though I have grown neither as wise nor as strong as Jesus did, I do have the grace of God upon me. Jesus himself convinced me of this by the way he lived his life among us. These lessons in God's love assure me every time that my loved ones will be fine after all. You see, God's grace is upon us all.

> *Good and Gracious God, I thank You for the grace in all of our lives. Your Presence enhances our best efforts and softens our sinfulness. You draw goodness even from our imperfections.*

The Seventh Day of Christmas
December 31

"No one has ever seen God. It is God the only Son, ever at the Father's side, who has revealed God."
From John 1:1-18

My long past teaching days taught me to make the most of our winter breaks. My husband, our sons and I filled this time away from school with everything that our school schedules kept us from. We played in the snow and went to movies to get out of the cold. Enjoying new toys and other Christmas gifts added to the fun. We went to bed a little later and slept a little later with great relish.

This New Year's Eve, our sons and their wives and kids are making the most of this break from their jobs and preschool. I cannot help smiling as I acknowledge that this particular family tradition was not lost on the younger generation. They learned well to appreciate one another, and they're teaching their children the same.

God, You revealed Yourself to us through Jesus. Help us to reveal You as well in the precious moments we share with one another today and throughout the coming year.

Something To Think About...

The Feast of the Holy Family
New Year's Day

"When the pair had fulfilled all the prescriptions of the law of the Lord, they returned to Galilee and their own town of Nazareth."
From Luke 2:22-40

After breakfast, I allowed myself a moment in the living room to sit before our family Christmas Tree and the village and crèche that rest beneath it. My earliest memories include similar scenes in my parents' home and the homes of numerous family members. Our Christmas Trees simply weren't complete without the little town of Bethlehem nestled at their feet. Though I began this tradition in our home the first Christmas we were married, my husband and our sons took over this task early on. Though Mike and Tim have moved on to their own homes and their own Christmas Trees, their dad continues to serve as village planner in this house. As for me, I unpack the boxes and step back as my dear husband lies before the tree to fashion the current year's scene.

As I studied my husband's handiwork this particular Christmas, it occurred to me that the peace and joy that we associate with the first Christmas likely graced Mary and Joseph much differently than the scene before me suggested. Mary and Joseph didn't choose Bethlehem to be the birthplace of their son. Caesar Augustus required all citizens to return to their own cities to register for a census. Since Joseph's roots were in Bethlehem, he and his wife were compelled to travel there. When the couple arrived, Bethlehem teemed with people who'd made the same journey for the same purpose. When Joseph failed to find a place to stay, a compassionate innkeeper led him and Mary to his livestock shelter. They would find some privacy there as Mary's labor progressed. Though a warm room and a clean bed escaped them, Mary and Joseph gave thanks for what they had been given as they prepared to welcome Jesus into their lives. Not much later, something in the sky alerted nearby shepherds to a baby's cry in the night. It was to these outcasts that Mary and Joseph first introduced their child. Though many would consider themselves far more worthy than these shepherds to greet the Messiah, God chose the shepherds to welcome Jesus to his life among us.

It seems that the difficult circumstances that surrounded Jesus' birth were a small taste of the hardships to come for the Holy Family. The Magi traveled a great distance as they followed the star that heralded this new king. Though Mary and Joseph certainly thanked God for this wondrous visit, they likely followed their prayer of thanks with a prayer for counsel. How would they raise this amazing child? Not long after the Magi's departure, an angel's warning came in answer to their prayer. God's messenger warned Joseph of King Herod's wrath and instructed him to flee to Egypt with Mary and the child. There they remained until Herod's death. Though Joseph intended to return to their home, a second angel warned them of another tyrant who is the reason Joseph finally settled his family in Nazareth.

As I stared at the little Bethlehem that rested under our Christmas Tree, I shuddered as reality's chill took hold of me. Though many shared joyful and peaceful moments before this tree, our little village and crèche, life in the world around us continues with all of its imperfections, hardship and pain. It seems to me that this is the message of today's Feast of the Holy Family. Though Joseph and Mary nurtured Jesus, our Savior and King, their holy family wasn't spared the difficulties that too often punctuate life on this earth. Though God showered them with loving care for all the days of their lives, God also allowed them the freedom to make the best of their lot as only they could. The two thousand years since bear witness to the fruits of Joseph's and Mary's efforts. Our hearts would never have been touched by Jesus' message if Mary and Joseph hadn't done their parts.

You know, God fashioned your circumstances and mine with even more loving care than my husband expended as he fashioned the little village under our Christmas Tree. God gave Mary and Joseph all that they needed to nurture Jesus and one another in the worst of circumstances, and God does the same for you and me. Jesus, Mary and Joseph aren't the only holy family that we celebrate today. Indeed, God's presence among us makes each of our families holy as well. By this reading, you've experienced the best and worst of this Christmas, just as Mary and Joseph experienced the best and worst of the First Christmas. Like them, we turn to God in both cases -to offer our thanks and to seek God's counsel. Like them, we simply do our part as only we can.

Mary and Joseph, on this first day of the New Year, we celebrate you. God dwelled in your midst, yet you embraced life in this world as we do. Keep us mindful of God's presence among us. Each day of this New Year, help us to embrace the lives we've been given just as you did —with great faith and absolute trust in God's plans for us.

Something To Think About...

The Ninth Day of Christmas - January 2

*"I am 'a voice in the desert, crying out:
Make straight the way of the Lord!'"
From John 1:19-28*

It seems to me that we begin every New Year with great expectations of ourselves and those around us. Our hopes may include finally reaching that ideal weight, giving up cigarettes or overcoming an addiction that may not be hurting others, but that certainly has taken its toll on our own hearts. Whatever our imperfections, the New Year provides another opportunity to try once again to better ourselves.

Years of disappointment have convinced me that I improve myself best when I forget about me. When I begin anew focused on this world of ours and those whom I've been given to love, my energy increases. I spend my time and myself on those who need me. Sometimes, my efforts are life-changing. Sometimes, my efforts are only moment-changing. Always, my efforts change me for the better.

> *Jesus, my teacher and guide, your life offers the greatest lessons in living for others. Help me to see my circumstances and those around me with your eyes and help me to make the best of both.*

The Tenth Day of Christmas - January 3

*"Now I have seen for myself and have testified,
'This is God's chosen One.'"
From John 1:29-34*

A very wise teacher once told me that if I ever wanted to know whether or not a person was a good soul simply to watch how children react to him or her. Though I wasn't necessarily convinced of Sister Imelda's wisdom at the time, three decades of working with children and my own parenting experience have supported her assertion. Children somehow instinctively seem to know who does and who does not have their best interest at heart.

My sons, Mike and Tim, instinctively seemed to know a lot of things. When my parenting came from the heart, they complied with my wishes with little or no complaint. However, when I pushed them in directions that I myself wasn't sold on, they baulked. They kept me honest in many ways, helping me to keep my words and deeds in sync.

> *Patient Jesus, you opened yourself to everyone you met along the way. The only ones you seemed to have difficulty with were the hypocrites who held themselves above everyone else. This New Year, help me to know my own heart and yours more intimately and help me to live accordingly.*

Something To Think About...

The Eleventh Day of Christmas
January 4

*"Let the sea and what fills it resound,
the world and those who dwell in it;
Let rivers clap their hands,
the mountains shout with them for joy
before the Lord."
From Psalm 98, 1:7-9*

Every winter captivates me with its onslaught of snow and cold. I find nothing more beautiful than an ice-clad tree or an undisturbed expanse of hardened snow. Add the crunch of that snow under my feet and a chilling wind around me, and I'm in heaven! I willingly volunteer to be the driver in the worst winter weather. Even then, I find peace in the midst of nature's havoc.

Why this affinity with this difficult season? Perhaps winter, when most living things lie dormant beneath the surface, symbolizes the potential to be found in so many unexpected places -and people. Perhaps knowing that spring will eventually come inspires my hope that, indeed, life is everywhere. Everywhere and in everyone!

Creator God, thank you for the beauty of this world that so inspires my hope. Help me to uncover that hope for those around me, whatever the season.

The Twelfth Day of Christmas
January 5

"This, remember, is the message you heard from the beginning: we should love one another."
From 1 John 3:11-21

A storm is brewing just beyond my window. What an odd phenomenon to hear thunder before a snow. If my minimal meteorological knowledge serves me, I should expect ice pellets, rather than snowflakes, to fall within the next few minutes.

It occurs to me that my knowledge of human nature far exceeds what I know about the weather. Still, I sometimes ignore this wisdom and "push buttons" that would best be left alone. Though I know well what will come next if I attempt to have the last word, I speak in spite of myself. Though the thunder threatens, I push when I should let go and let love take care.

Gentle Jesus, you suffered the worst of what we humans can inflict upon one another. During this season of new beginnings, help me to see with your eyes and feel with your heart. Help me respond to every storm with a rainbow of love.

Something To Think About...

Christmas Weekday - January 6

*"I have written this to make you realize
that you possess eternal life..."
From 1 John 5:5-13*

One of the most enjoyable things I do is to write a weekly reflection for my parish church bulletin. This began twenty years ago when our founding pastor determined that we must function as a "real parish" from the beginning. Father Farrell rented a school gym where we'd celebrate Mass, had a portable altar made, borrowed vestments from another parish and prepared our first Sunday Bulletin. After filling a few pages, Father realized that lots of white space remained. It was then that he invited me, a teacher and the deacon's wife, to write "something inspirational that will fill a column or two."

Every week since, I've poured over the scriptures and my own life experiences to find ways to spread the word – not my word, but the Good News that God's Spirit has so generously revealed to me. Truly, I can't help myself. What God has shared is simply too good to keep inside!

> *O Holy Spirit, thank You for inspiring my writing. Inspire all of the moments of our lives. Help us to serve one another by sharing our talents through our labor and our leisure, in good times and in times of sorrow.*

Christmas Weekday - January 7

*"We have this confidence in God:
that God hears us whenever we ask for anything..."*
From 1 John 5:14-21

It was New Year's Day, and my mom was staying with us over the holidays. When she didn't get up for breakfast, I went to her room and found her to be ill. She suffered a high fever and had no appetite. She spent the day in bed, unable to eat or drink much of anything. What little she did consume didn't stay with her for long.

Over the next fourteen hours, we went through several sets of linens and nightclothes. By 9:00 P.M., I found myself quite impatient that the Lord God had not yet made my mother well. At 10:45 P.M., I stormed out the front door with a last bit of trash for the next morning's garbage pick-up. I looked up to a most beautiful star-studded sky and raised my clenched fist to the Almighty. "This is your sister," I bellowed, "and you can make her well if you want to!" With that, I returned to my mother's room where she lay sleeping peacefully, her fever completely gone.

Forgiving God, though I know You forgave me before I even asked, again, I say I'm sorry. Help me never to doubt that You know our needs before we do and that You fulfill them far more lovingly than we would ever dare to expect.

The Feast of the Epiphany - January 8

"They were overjoyed at seeing the star, and on entering the house they saw the child with Mary his mother. They prostrated themselves in homage. They opened their treasures and offered him gifts of gold, frankincense and myrrh."
From Matthew 2:1-12

It was New Year's Day, several years ago, when I mentioned to my sister, Rita, that we would probably take down our Christmas Tree during the coming week. A somewhat horrified look replaced the smile she'd worn all day as she asked, "Why would you do that?" Rita went on to remind me that the Three Kings would not arrive until the Feast of the Epiphany and that our family has NEVER taken down the Christmas Tree before then. Having been sufficiently reprimanded, I eased away from the subject by recalling our parents' experience with their Christmas Tree the year they were married.

It was just two months after my parents' were married when their first Christmas together arrived. They had hardly completed their thank you notes from the wedding when it occurred to them that is was time to prepare for Christmas. Together, they determined that the Christmas Season provided a wonderful opportunity to welcome family and friends to their new apartment. As a result, the two of them set out to do just that. They purchased and decorated the perfect tree. Regardless of the opinions of others, they were convinced this was the most beautiful tree either had ever seen. When the decorating was completed and their apartment looked just right, they began to invite family and friends to their new little home.

For weeks and weeks, their free time was filled with parents, brothers and sisters, aunts and uncles, cousins and friends whom they happily entertained. My mother admitted that it was April when she and our dad finally finished what they set out to do. By that time, their very dry, almost needle-free Christmas Tree had become a part of the apartment they came to know as "home." My mother was heartbroken when she and my dad finally forced themselves to dispose of it. In the years that followed, a bit of that same sorrow appeared on my mother's face each time the calendar dictated that it was time to take down our Christmas Tree.

Neither of my parents were the hopeless sentimentalists that their first Christmas as husband and wife suggests. Indeed, they were very practical people who looked life squarely in the face. This was especially true each time tragedy touched them. They managed to survive, I believe, because they were people of great faith. Somehow, they held tightly to those few truths that are important to us all. Through their Christmas observances, my parents acknowledged the miracle of God's participation in human history. That first holy night, this precious moment was celebrated again and again in the arrivals of the angels and the shepherds, and, later, in the arrival of the Magi from the East. Just as my parents rejoiced with each new guest who arrived at their door, so God rejoices each time we gather to recognize and celebrate that, indeed, God dwells among us.

My parents waited long after the arrival of the Magi to remove the signs of Christmas 1942 from their home.

Something To Think About...

They kept their Yuletide trimmings intact until every possible person had enjoyed them. This is precisely what the God of Moses and Abraham did by extending knowledge of the Messiah to those outside of God's beloved Jewish Community. The signs observed by the astrologers from the East were an invitation to all the world to come and to witness the arrival of Jesus. They were also an invitation to embrace the promise that this arrival holds for us all.

Our observance of the Epiphany of the Lord is the completion of our observance of Christmas. Christ's birth takes on its true significance when it is shared with all of humankind. The Epiphany of the Lord is a celebration of God among us. Our challenge is to recognize that "us" includes anyone and everyone whom we encounter as we journey through this life. Just as my mom and dad extended their Christmas hospitality to everyone they knew for as long as it took, God invites us to do the same for everyone we come to know for as long as it takes.

God Among Us, we are present day Magi, invited to follow the star of faith as we journey home to You. Just as the Magi shared the joy of your birth with their people, help us to share Your Presence with everyone we meet, today and throughout this New Year.

Monday After the Epiphany - January 9

"They carried to him all those afflicted with various diseases and racked with pain: the possessed, the lunatics, the paralyzed. He cured them all."
From Matthew 4:12-17, 23-25

The realities of winter and our daily routines have returned in full force. This holiday season brought new losses and memories of too many loved ones passed. Though our certainty in the current bliss of these dear souls remains steadfast, the sting of their departures remains as well. Daily routines tend to soften such emotions. Still, my husband's work as a hospice chaplain has added to the melancholy at our house.

When the people we love are sick, it's difficult to see God's hand in their suffering. When depression, addiction or a misguided heart brings them pain, we wonder why. The scriptures teem with examples of the healing powers of Jesus, and we ask why not now?

When I find myself struggling with these questions, I look to Jesus who hung on a cross and endured his suffering. Jesus knew what was coming afterward, and he determined that eternal life for us all was worth the trouble. Aren't our troubles worth it as well?

> *Amazing Jesus, you became human to show us that the best of this life is only a taste of what comes afterward. Thank you!*

Something To Think About...

Tuesday After the Epiphany - January 10

"Jesus saw a vast crowd. He pitied them, for they were like sheep without a shepherd; and he began to teach them at great length."
From Matthew 6:34-44

I worked as a reading teacher for many years. Though the subject area remained constant, my students' grade levels varied as a result of my assignment, enrollment numbers and sometimes the whims of the powers that be. For a few years, I worked with only fifth through eighth graders. While I tended to enjoy all of my students, one group of eighth graders remains a favorite.

For some reason this particular group needed an adult ear. Every day when they reported to my classroom, they attempted to share their woes for the entire period. The truth is that they actually weren't engaging in work avoidance. One of their classmates had unexpectedly lost his dad. This turned my students' world upside down. They simply couldn't cope. So it was that we came to an agreement. We spent ten minutes of each period sharing and thirty-five minutes of each period reading. Apparently, they appreciated this gesture because they'd both calmed down and learned something by the end of the year.

Just as you taught us, Jesus, sometimes we have to adjust the rules to serve a soul. Please give us the wisdom and the love to know how and when.

Wednesday After the Epiphany
January 11

*"Then, seeing them tossed about
as they tried to row with the wind against them,
he came walking toward them on the water."
From Matthew 6:45-52*

Terrible!! Horrible! How can she hurt these children that way? Though I couldn't remember ever writing off a single day of my life, this is precisely what I wished for. I needed to go back to one minute before midnight and start over. Perhaps then I could prevent this impending injustice.

After two wonderfully successful years of planning and implementing an extremely successful reading program that brought success to those most likely to fail, one of the powers that be reneged on an agreement. I would not be given three years to prove the staff's and program's worth in spite of the fact that test scores already reflected extremely positive outcomes.

I left my office because of the darkness that loomed over me there. When I entered the corridor, I didn't notice a soul. A teacher later asked me why I ignored her greeting. At the moment tears threatened to overwhelm me, a small voice intervened. "Hi, Mrs. Spinach. I'm coming to your class today, right?" Of course he was!

Jesus, my Savior, who knew that you'd come in such a small voice to rescue me that day? Thank you for inspiring my courage with a call to serve.

Something To Think About...

Thursday After the Epiphany
January 12

*"God has sent me to bring glad tidings to the poor,
to proclaim liberty to captives, recovery of sight to the blind,
and release to prisoners..."*
From Luke 4:14-22

Our community is blessed with many generous people, some of whom support and staff two local food pantries. Though the level of services available differs between the two, both do an amazingly effective job of feeding the needy who come to their doors. What touched me most when I visited these facilities were the joyful attitudes of those who worked with clients. Everything these volunteers said and did indicated that they had absolutely nothing better to do than to minister to each person with whom they interacted. The smiles on the faces of those served reflected the kindness with which they were met.

After Christmas, as our holiday spirit dwindles, so do food donations to these pantries. Today, I'll tweak our budget enough to find something to help.

> *Generous Jesus, you offer us a glimpse of heaven's bliss when we care for one another. Inspire us to share our gifts generously, just as you did, with those most in need.*

Friday After the Epiphany - January 13

"'Lord, if you will do so, you can cure me.'
Jesus stretched out his hand to touch him
and said, 'I will do it. Be cured.'"
From Luke 5:12-16

When I was a little girl, my parents convinced me that it is always appropriate to bring our troubles to God. Sometimes, we did so en masse. We gathered in our living room to recite the Rosary when my Uncle Gee suffered a bout with pneumonia. We prayed for his recovery every night. When it became clear that this was not in the offing, we prayed that his would be a happy death.

Those prayerful gatherings and my parents' seemingly familiar stance toward the Lord God encouraged me to speak plainly and directly in my prayer. Though I'd like to think that I've refined my approach a bit, I still find myself speaking with the Almighty as I would with my best friend. I never wonder if God is listening. Why question the obvious?

> *Dear God, You attend to each one of us every moment of every day. Fill our hearts with the generosity of spirit to emulate Your devotion in our relationships with one another.*

Saturday After the Epiphany
January 14

*"That is my joy, and it is complete.
He must increase, while I must decrease."
From John 3:22-30*

From the time I realized what a nun was, I wanted to enter the convent. I remember cleaning house with my mom. As we worked, I asked her opinion of some "sister names" I'd come up with. "I could be Sister Mary Raoul Rita or Sister Raoul Marie. Maybe they'd let me have Sister Rita Raoul." I'd fixated on my dad's name as he'd recently passed away. I included my mom's name in the mix as a show of my support of her in this life without my dad.

Though I spent a lot of time with the sisters over the years, including an entire summer during college, I never did become one of them. Oddly, it was during that summer that the sisters encouraged me to accept a date with the young man who eventually became my husband.

In spite of my marital state, the call to service has remained. Both my husband and I have found amazing and unexpected ways to make God's work our own.

> *Jesus, you made God's work your own when you embraced your life among us. In everything you did, you revealed the Divine. Help me to lose myself in service to those you have given me to love.*

The Baptism of the Lord - January 15
*"You are my beloved son.
On you my favor rests."
From Mark 1:7-11*

Though the approach of Valentine's Day is already apparent in many stores, this is the day that the Church closes the Christmas Season, just as we have at home. At our house, my husband deals with the outdoor decorations, while I tend to the Christmas Tree inside. Every year, I find myself reluctant to do so. Since our sons are both married and join their wives in decorating their own homes, I decorate our annual tree myself. In the process, I can't help becoming rather fond of these beautiful firs.

Though I decorate myself, I never do so alone. I place my treasured copy of It's a Wonderful Life into the DVD player and raise the television volume in the family room just enough to allow me to hear the dialogue in the living room. All the while, I work in the company of George Bailey and the many people to whom George's life made all of the difference in the world. When my poor husband comes in from the invariable cold, George Bailey's wonderful life is the last thing that concerns him. Life's meaning isn't of particular interest as he attempts to warm himself. I usually urge him into his recliner with the hope that a short nap will dull his memory of the freezing outdoors. In the end, Mike always dozes off, and I return to my work with George Bailey and company to urge me along...

Though I can only hear the dialogue of the movie,

images of George Bailey's life fill me up. The succession of selfless decisions that have become George's life draws frequent tears from me. Though I know precisely how the movie will end, I suffer every disappointment with George as though I have no idea that things will work themselves out. "Poor courageous George," I think to myself. "If only he realized just how good he is!" And so it goes until the movie ends and my one-time Christmas Tree is bare.

Each year, I have a hard time committing our tree to the parkway. There it waits for a public works employee to toss it unceremoniously into a truck for the trip to the land of mulch. As I stare at the tree, I acknowledge that George Bailey felt much like that tree far more often than he should have. George should have felt good about the wonderful things he had done for others. He saved his brother's life and that of a sick child who was sent the wrong medicine by a distraught pharmacist. He took over his father's business to prevent the loss of many jobs and many more homes. He sent his brother off to college in his own place. All the while, he fought temptation in the form of Mr. Potter, the most miserly man in town, to stand up for God's "riff raff." Yes, George Bailey was a good, good man who gave the working poor and many others something to live for. Finally, when George felt that he had no more to give, the God of the "riff raff" stepped in through Clarence, the bumbling angel-to-be. Go ahead. Watch the movie for yourself. Join George for a celebration of what truly was a wonderful life. For this is the point of today's observance of the Baptism of the Lord.

The gospels tell us that John the Baptist is deeply

inspired by the things Jesus has said and done. When Jesus asks to be baptized, John is reluctant to cooperate, for John feels it is Jesus who should baptize him. Jesus asks John to be the baptizer just the same. After John immerses Jesus in the waters of the Jordan River, God enters into the scene to announce to all who will hear, "You are my beloved son. On you my favor rests."

These words, proclaimed from the heavens over Jesus, are meant just as readily for John the Baptist, for the George Baileys among us, for you and for me. Though they don't echo for us from the clouds above, we hear them just as clearly in the depths of our hearts. These words resound each and every time we embrace the difficult and selfless choices that make all of the difference in the world to those we have been given to love. When we feel we have no more to give, like George who was tempted to hurl himself off that bridge, God steps in. Though God's appearance may not always be as endearing as that of Clarence, it is far more real and absolutely lasting.

I chuckle in spite of myself over the many tears I shed each time I watch It's a Wonderful Life. I know how the film will end, yet I cry through it every time. This phenomenon repeated itself in the reality of Jesus' life. Jesus prayed often. Jesus revealed God's love in his actions toward those who needed him and in stories like the Parable of the Prodigal Son. Jesus knew that all would end well. Still, the suffering, disappointment and discouragement along the way weren't easy. The same is true for you and me.

Though our faith tells us that all will be well in the

end, we fret and suffer so. Selfless choices aren't easy to make, and, when we fail to see the value of what we do, we find ourselves on that bridge with George Bailey. It seems to me that it is when we are on that bridge that we must remember George's joy when his life is given back to him. It is when we are on that bridge that we must recall God's words at the baptism of Jesus and realize that they are meant for us as well... "You are my beloved. On you my favor rests." It is when we are on that bridge that we must passionately acknowledge that we live for the happy ending that will become the happiest beginning we will ever know!

> *Patient Lord, you lived your life among us teaching us to put others first. You repeated this lesson in everything you said and did. Make us good students who discover the joy of caring for others again and again.*

Monday - January 16

*"Jesus said to them, 'Come after me;
I will make you fishers of men.' They immediately abandoned
their nets and became his followers."*
From Mark 1:14-20

God's story drew me in when I was very young, probably before I entered kindergarten. It seems reasonable to attribute this phenomenon to my parents who took our faith to heart. Though money was tight in our house, my mom purchased a family bible series which arrived in monthly installments. Each edition included a book from the bible with colorful artwork that brought its stories to life. I recall pouring over the pages with my younger sisters. Years later, when my teachers referenced the scriptures during religion class, images from that bible resurfaced, bringing their lessons to life.

When I consider how quickly the disciples walked away from everything to follow Jesus, I wonder what it was that drew them in. Simon and Andrew seemed to be strong, burly, hard-working men. Still, they left their livelihoods to follow Jesus. Perhaps this God-made-man couldn't contain the wonder within him. Perhaps just being nearby was enough to draw people to Jesus. When I consider the Jesus I've come to know, I understand the attraction.

Dear Jesus, thank you for the gift of yourself. You have transformed my life from the moment I first heard your name.

Tuesday - January 17
Feast of St. Anthony, Abbot

"He is able to deal patiently with the ignorant and erring, for he himself is beset by weakness."
From Hebrews 5:1-10

My brother is a bit of a character. I recall my parents' "discussions" with him when he'd come home late for dinner or had forgotten to take out the trash again. Still, from the time he was a kid, my brother also did the most unexpected things to be helpful.

Though Raoul was only fourteen when we lost our dad, he helped by taking a job at the corner store. He earned ten dollars each week by delivering groceries with his wagon. He kept one dollar for himself and gave the rest to our mom. Raoul often provided me and my friends with rides to movies or the bowling alley. Ours was a blue collar neighborhood where no work meant no pay. During Chicago's Snowstorm of '67, my brother dug out his car and then drove up and down Chicago Avenue providing people rides to their jobs. Once, when he'd witnessed a car accident, Raoul directed traffic around the scene until the police arrived. Later, when my brother's bout with diabetes resulted in dialysis, he became the life of the party during those long hours of treatment. When Raoul passed away, his fellow patients mourned his loss along with us.

Thank you, Jesus, for my brother and the good souls like him who so creatively brighten our lives.

Wednesday - January 18

"Let us move on to the neighboring villages so that I may proclaim the good news there also. That is what I have come to do."
From Mark 1:29-39

Our neighbor, Ellie, became an auxiliary grandma to our son Mike from the day he was born. Because she lived next door, Mike saw Ellie every day. When she'd relax on her patio after a long day of teaching, Ellie always had a snack and some juice for the little guy who'd wander over. I admit that I benefited from Ellie's friendship at least as much as my son did.

Mike was just seven years old. He wasn't at all happy with what I'd asked him to do, and he shouted "I hate you!" I never used that word myself, and it broke my heart to hear it from my little boy. I remained calm until Mike's bedroom door slammed and then the tears flowed. When I went out to our backyard to recover, I saw Ellie. Still teary-eyed, I told her what had happened. "Did your kids ever say that?" I asked. "Sure they did. They're kids. And you know what I did? I pulled them close and said, 'Well, that's okay because I still love you!'" Ellie added that this gesture quickly put an end to such talk. Mike repeated his comment only once more, probably because I followed Ellie's lead to a tee.

Dear Jesus, your good news makes good sense always and everywhere. Thank you for sharing so much of your good news through Ellie.

Something To Think About...

Thursday - January 19

"It was no longer possible for Jesus to enter a town openly. He stayed in desert places; yet people kept coming to him from all sides."
From Mark 1:40-45

My husband was ordained a deacon almost twenty-four years ago. All the while, he's served locally in our own parish. As a result, Mike meets people he knows whenever he's out and about here in Gurnee. Several years ago, our son Tim began to take notice of all of these "Deacon Mike Sightings". Whenever he was here and Mike returned home, Tim asked, "So, who'd you see today?" This father-son joke became more hilarious when Mike told Tim that we ran into fellow parishioners at a rest stop on our way to visit him at the University of Illinois in Champaign, at an eatery in Wisconsin Dells and on The Strip in Las Vegas.

We laugh because Mike's face has become a familiar local fixture, and we're grateful for this development as well. Mike's approachability and availability have welcomed many who might otherwise not have sought out help when they needed it most. Thank you, Dear! Keep up the good work!

Compassionate Jesus, I offer an extra prayer for my husband today. Keep his heart open to those who need him, and fill him up with the grace he needs to respond as you would.

Friday - January 20
St. Fabian and St. Sebastian

"As for you, every hair of your head has been counted; so do not be afraid of anything."
From Matthew 10:28-33

I will always be grateful for the amazing authors I met in college. Though these weren't face-to-face encounters, they were certainly life-changing. Elisabeth Kübler-Ross pioneered near-death experience studies. I read her work for a class on death and dying. The good doctor's scientific research regarding life after this life underscored what my faith had already convinced me was true. While she endured ridicule from others in her field, Kübler-Ross persisted. In the aftermath, many well respected medical professionals substantiated and added to her research.

I read Nobel Laureate and Holocaust survivor Elie Wiesel for philosophy class. This amazing man's stalwart spirit sustained him through one of human history's most heinous episodes. His endurance has inspired me during difficult times throughout my adult life.

These authors touched me with the amazing strength they exhibited in the face of adversity. In both cases, the truths they unveiled are worthy of consideration by us all.

Loving God, even Jesus met adversity along the way. Help me not to fear the bumps in the road ahead because You will walk over them or around them with me.

Something To Think About...

Saturday - January 21, Feast of St. Agnes

*"The moral is: keep your eyes open,
for you know not the day or hour."
From Matthew 25:1-13*

I expected to hear that her recovery might be lengthy, that her dementia might be increased by the anesthesia and that we needed to be prepared for a decline as our mom's body was growing tired. I didn't expect to hear about the cancer, her four-month life expectancy and the possibility of pain that might darken her perpetual smile. Then, we told our mother the news...

Mom shared our surprise at the diagnosis, but not at the outcome. "We all have to die from something. I've had a good long life. I wanted to leave an educated family that contributes, and I have. I hope I can do what I want for a while. I hope I can be comfortable. I hope I go without too much trouble. I hope..." I hoped, too.

Though the news was unexpected, the outcome was precisely what my mom had hoped for. God supplied the grace that sustained my mom throughout her final journey home. The pain never came. Mom did everything she hoped to until her last two days. On the day she left us, her eyes weren't open, but her heart was.

> *Patient God, one would think that by now I'd be prepared for life's surprises. Thank You for surrounding these events and us with the grace we need to endure.*

Second Sunday - January 22

*"As he watched Jesus walk by, he said,
'Look! There is the Lamb of God!'"*
From John 1:35-42

Aside from the sale items in a few stores, remnants of the Christmas Season are nowhere to be seen. Our crèche rests in storage with the carefully wrapped figures that brought the Nativity to life. The splashes of red foliage that proclaimed Christmas so dramatically in our parish church have given way to a new liturgical season. Until Ash Wednesday, we'll observe Ordinary Time.

It seems to me that "ordinary" is a misnomer that gives the wrong impression of the time that fills the weeks surrounding the Christmas and Easter Seasons. Though these seasons celebrate Jesus' entrance into and departure from human history, they mark only a fraction of the events that make up Jesus' life. Indeed, Jesus' conception, birth, death and resurrection embody the greatest mysteries of our faith. Still, what speaks poignantly to me is the tremendous love evident in Jesus' interactions with those he encounters each and every day between his birth and death.

I suppose none of us would be reading this reflection or observing Ordinary Time if we didn't feel called to do so in some way. Perhaps we're attending to things spiritual in answer to a sense of guilt or to pressure from our spouses. Perhaps this is a response to the responsibility we have to our children or to the comfort we find in the familiar. Perhaps it is our own need that prompts us to attend to our souls. Whatever the reason, we feel compelled to participate in the spiritual dimension of this life. In my case and most of yours, this includes involvement with God and our faith community. This participation may be limited to attending church occasionally. It may be as far-reaching as inviting God into every moment of our lives. I suspect most of our efforts fall somewhere between the two. Whatever the case, our past isn't of concern today. On this particular day, you and I are invited to "up the ante" by opening ourselves a bit more to the presence of God in our lives.

If you're like I am, you need encouragement as you reflect upon God's call. Fortunately, the scriptures offer us some reassurance. 1 Samuel (3:3b-10, 19) tells us Samuel's story. He's the young man whom God calls several times before Samuel recognizes the voice that he hears. In the end, Samuel answers God's call, and God rewards this response by remaining present to Samuel throughout his life.

1 Corinthians (6:13c-15a, 17-20) tells us Paul's story. Paul has reflected greatly since his conversion. Paul has come to realize that not only our spirits, but our bodies as well are to be spent in answering God's call. Which of our gifts is more ordinary and human than our bodies, yet capable of such tremendous goodness? The mass of flesh and bone that constitutes our presence to others is also the most effective means we have to bring God to one another.

If you're not yet convinced that our imperfect selves can indeed respond competently to God, see John's gospel (1:35-42). As Jesus passes, John the Baptist calls to his

for Christmastime and Winter Days

followers, "Behold, the lamb of God." Two disciples say nothing, but they follow Jesus very closely. Not ever missing one of us, Jesus notices the pair and asks what they're looking for. They answer with their own question, "Where are you staying?" So begins the relationship that will change all of their lives -and ours. Indeed, Andrew is so taken with Jesus that he calls his brother Simon to come along. Andrew knows that he's found the Messiah. In turn, Jesus is so taken with Andrew, his brother and all of his followers that he remains with them and loves them in everything, even in their desertion and denial of his friendship.

Though I fully appreciate the wonder of the Christmas and Easter Seasons, I find myself quite taken with Ordinary Time. This season, named for its ordinal arrangement of Sundays, avails us to Jesus' daily life when he did his best work among us.

In my own life, I long for ordinary days filled with expectations numerous enough to keep me busy, but few enough to keep me sane. I sometimes feel such days have escaped me forever. War assaults our world, loved ones find themselves overwhelmed with worry, and the trivia of daily living demands more and more attention. Yet, the persistent voice deep within me argues that times like these give meaning to our ordinary days, "...opportunities for imperfect humans to find just enough strength to love and to serve those who need them, just as Jesus did."

Now these are the persistent voice's words, and not my own. Because I suspect their Source, I won't argue with them. I'm reminded that Jesus turned the ordinary days of a carpenter-turned-apprentice preacher into extraordinary opportunities for humankind. Today, you and I are called to do the same, one ordinary moment after another.

Jesus, thank you for teaching as effectively with your actions as you did with your words. Thank you for transforming our meager efforts into the sacred. For it is through us that you minister to souls.

Monday - January 23

"'Why do John's disciples and those of the Pharisees fast while yours do not?' Jesus replied, 'How can the guests at a wedding fast as long as the groom is still among them?'"
From Mark 2:18-22

I used to have a difficult time at wakes. I didn't know how to express my sentiments to those who mourned. This began when my Uncle Gee lay on his deathbed. My dad softened the blow of his impending loss by sharing that Uncle Gee would be well in heaven. His polio-ravaged body would be straight and tall and he'd be very happy. Daddy's words served me well over the next few years when both of my grandpas and my dad himself passed away.

A lifetime of losses and an insatiable interest in life after this life have convinced me that my dad was correct in his assertion regarding Uncle Gee's future. Add to that all that Jesus revealed about God and the wonder that awaits us in heaven, and you see my problem. The truth is that every time I received news of a passing, including that of my mom, the first thing I did was congratulate heaven's newest arrival. Eventually, it occurred to me to also ask this soul to watch over those who mourn him or her. I realized that feeling the sting of loss doesn't lessen our faith in the things to come. It just hurts. This is when I finally knew what to say.

Loving God, bless those who mourn today and keep us all mindful of the things to come.

Tuesday - January 24
Feast of St. Francis de Sales

"Jesus said to his disciples, 'You are the salt of the earth...
You are the light of the world.'"
From Matthew 5:13-16

I clearly remember praying that day with my eyes wide open and a scowl on my face. At age sixteen, I'd decided that it wasn't at all fair that I had a vocation. At the time, we continually prayed for vocations to the priesthood and religious life, and I was convinced that God intended for me to join the convent. Still, I told the Lord God that I wanted to be a normal girl, with a normal life who might just get married one day. I said this in spite of the fact that I thought that our parish sisters and priests and my aunts who were nuns were perfectly normal.

Over the years since, I've frequently expressed my gratitude for being called at all. Jesus wasn't targeting the temple hierarchy, government officials, local celebrities or the wealthy when he proclaimed that we are the salt of the earth and the light of the world. Jesus holds each of us in such esteem that he calls us all, regardless of our status, to be the salt and the light that only we can be.

> *Creative God, thank You for giving each of us the power to make ourselves and one another better people and to make this world a better place. Help us to use that power with wisdom and love.*

Wednesday – January 25
Conversion of St. Paul

"Go into the whole world and proclaim the gospel to every creature."
From Matthew 16:15-18

Uncle Paul and his daughter Dawn lived in the first floor flat below us. He was my mom's handsome older brother and one of the first soldiers I'd ever met. My uncle worked hard as a carpenter by day and spent many of his evenings at the tavern across the street. Though I didn't understand the circumstances, I knew that he suffered from a broken heart. One day, Dawn shared that she and her boyfriend Richard wanted to get married. On another day, my uncle met Richard's mother. From that day on, my uncle spent his evenings with the new love of his life. He never crossed the street to that tavern again, and he did live happily ever after. Love truly transformed my uncle's life.

Whether we share ourselves in a lifelong relationship or in loving moments here and there, we proclaim the gospel just as Jesus asked.

> *God of love, help us to bring Your love to the people we meet along the way. Whether our encounters last a lifetime or only a few moments, let us all be better off because we met.*

Thursday - January 26
Feast St. Timothy and St. Titus

"...to Timothy, my dear child:
grace, mercy, and peace from God..."
From 2 Timothy 1:1-8

Dinner progressed as usual with talk about each of our days. In the midst of the conversation, our red-faced seven-year-old son suddenly howled, "Why am I the only one in this family whose name doesn't start with M?" My husband and I were taken aback because we had no idea that this so bothered our younger son. Before we could respond, Tim tearfully added, "Mike, Mary and Michael. Why is my name Timothy?" I decided that the only way to truly console our son was to tell him the truth.

"Tim, Dad's name was Mike and my name was Mary when we met. When we had our first baby and he was a boy, Dad wanted to name him after himself and Grandpa. So his name is Mike, too. When you were on the way, I just knew you were going to be a boy. Dad and I talked a lot about your name, but I didn't like any of the M names. Why pick a name just because of the M? I loved Timothy and that's why you have that name. Yours is the only name that this family really had to think about." With that, my smiling son Timothy finished his dinner.

Dear God, please bless all of Your children with grace, mercy and peace, especially those who are questioning their place in Your world today.

for Christmastime and Winter Days

Friday - January 27
Feast of St. Angela Merici

"Is a lamp brought in to be placed under a bushel basket or under a bed, and not to be placed on a lampstand?"
From Mark 4:21-25

Sometimes, we so underestimate our value to other people... As I prepared the reflections for this book, a publishing friend encouraged me to bring my correspondence up to date by utilizing a blog. The truth is that Larry set up the blog for me more than a year ago. Every week, he posts the weekly reflections I write for our parish bulletin and that I email to numerous other readers. Every week, when I receive Larry's post, I decide it's time to get that blog going. This past week, when I emailed the current article, I decided to poll my readers. I asked if they wished to continue to receive the articles, if they would mind doing so via a blog and if they preferred the email contact. Within an hour, my mailbox overflowed with responses. Regardless of their preferred medium, each one assured me that they wished to receive my weekly articles. I admit that I was completely awed by this fan mail.

I guess I'd better keep writing and get to that blog!

Thank you, Lord, for the fellow souls who open themselves up to my writing each week and for their generous encouragement. Thank You for all of the good people who take the time to encourage others.

Saturday - January 28
Feast of St. Thomas Aquinas

"With many such parables he spoke the word to them as they were able to understand it."
From Mark 4:26-34

In his capacity as deacon, my husband preaches at our Sunday Masses about once per month. The truth is that Mike is a very good homilist. He seems to touch the hearts of those who hear him as evidenced in the many positive comments he receives after Mass. The rest of the truth is that Mike spends weeks preparing for each of these talks. Regardless of the many compliments he receives, Mike never takes these opportunities to speak for granted. He struggles and reflects and rethinks until he's half-convinced that he's ready. This means that he's come up with a story that illustrates what he perceives to be the intent of the scriptures. Only after he's completed his last homily for the weekend is he somewhat convinced that he was ready after all. I think this bit of uncertainty keeps Mike on his toes. It helps him to be more creative than he ever dreamed possible.

> *Dear God, thank You for Mike and for all those who spread Your good news. Bless them with the inspiration they need to do justice to Your message. Bless all of us with receptive hearts, that we may attend to Your word wherever we encounter it.*

The Third Sunday - January 29

"This is the time of fulfillment.
The kingdom of God is at hand."
From Mark 1:14-20

As a child, I took my parents' words very seriously, mostly because they were illustrated so beautifully by their actions. To me, my dad was the most handsome and wonderful gentleman in the world because he behaved as such. His love for my mom was evident whenever they were together. Much of what I know about love, I learned from their relationship.

My mom seemed never to tire, always busy with something that needed to be done. Though I didn't know the term at the time, I truly admired her work ethic. She seemed to do whatever she did with enthusiastic dedication. Much of what I know about work, I learned from my mom.

As I grew older, I came to understand that my parents took God's presence in their lives very seriously as well. Their ability to love and nurture one another and their six children seems to have flowed from an underlying commitment to "be good". No matter where they found themselves, they responded as best they could by doing the right thing. Every situation, every moment of every day, represented a call to action. The wonder of their lives is that they listened to even the most muted calls, and they responded.

I suppose I've spent much of my life listening for God's call. As a child, it was easy. When I did as my parents asked, I was good. When I went to school and did what came naturally (Yes, I mean sitting at my desk with my hands folded and hanging upon Sister's every word.), I was good. When I entered junior high school, this became a bit more difficult. Though I continued to hear God's call, I resented listening to it. When I was teased about doing my homework or raising my hand in class, I wondered why I always had to be one of the good kids. Just once, I wanted one of the eighth grade boys who would be shaving soon to notice that I was sitting across the aisle from him. Foolish adolescent that I was, I failed to acknowledge free will. For a few miserable months, I forgot that it was I who had chosen to be good. Thank heaven I never fully lost sight of the reality that I actually liked being good. Indeed, I was pleased that God found the time to call me.

By the time I began high school, I heard God's call everywhere. I embraced the changes in the liturgy that came in the wake of Vatican II with opened arms. I could be found at any guitar Mass or prayer service belting out the hymns in English with all of my might. I protested lettuce growers who abused migrant workers, and I helped to provide religious education classes for special children. While in college, I added political action and work with the children of immigrants to my repertoire of answers to that call. In my mind, the greater the cause, the more important was my response.

Reality set in thirty-eight years ago when I married Mike. After uttering a simple "I do", I found myself called twenty-four hours a day to love a person I really didn't know very well. I'm sure the poor man had no idea of what he was getting himself into either. Though I remembered bits and pieces of my parents' lessons in love, I wasn't a quick study. My marriage didn't seem as perfect to me as their marriage had been. Obviously, the bits and pieces I'd remembered weren't the most important ones. It took many, many months for me to realize that I'd heard God's most important call to me in a proposal of marriage. For the first time, I'd been entrusted solely with the life of another. Similar calls came twice more at the births of our sons. How blessed my life became when I finally learned to listen to the calls that mattered most.

This truly is the time of fulfillment –today, this last Sunday in January of the New Year. The kingdom of God, wondrous as it is, is at hand. Just now for me, God's kingdom rests in my husband and our sons, Mike and Tim. God's kingdom rests in our daughters-in-law, Abby and Kim, and our three granddaughters, Ellie, Lauren and Claire. God's kingdom rests in Mike's brother and his family. God's kingdom rests in my sisters, their husbands and all of our nieces and nephews. God's kingdom rests in amazing lifelong friends like Trino and Scott. God's kingdom also rests in the many friends we've been blessed with along the way in our neighborhoods, at our workplaces and in our parish family. All of these special people who welcome us into their lives support us more than they'll ever know.

The same is true for you. God's kingdom also rests in those you have been given to love. As you prepare your own list of family and friends, in-laws and out-laws, don't engage in my foolishness, wasting precious time wondering why things are as they are. All we need to know is this: For a little while, we are each entrusted with the life of another. Whether our association is but a few seconds or lifelong, we are given that person to nurture and to care for. This is God's call... to love.

Dear God, I've finally learned that Your kingdom is everywhere around me and within everyone around me. Help me to see every encounter with another soul as an opportunity to celebrate and to share Your love.

for Christmastime and Winter Days

Monday - January 30

"I have found David, my servant; with my holy oil I have anointed him, that my hand may always be with him, and that my arm may make him strong."
From Psalm 28:20-26

I come from a very large family. My dad is one of twelve children, and my mom is one of eight. My earliest memories include large family gatherings for the holidays, christenings, birthdays, graduations, weddings and funerals. I grew up down the block from our church, so numerous people passed our house on the way to Mass each week. I worked at a grocery store throughout high school and college. Afterward, I married, began my teaching career and became involved in our parish church. Throughout all of this, people of every sort have come into my life.

I'm especially grateful for the moments I've shared individually with those around me. During these encounters, I received glimpses of many amazing souls. Several of them, especially my students, had no idea of their ability to contribute to this world of ours. I took great pleasure in pointing out their unique gifts. King David isn't God's only anointed one. Because we are God's children, we are anointed, too. Each of us is sent out to bless those around us and to bless this world with the gift of our self.

Thank you, Dear God, for loving us so much that You trust us to bring You into this world!

Something To Think About...

Tuesday - January 31
Feast of St. John Bosco

"Go home to your family and announce to them all that the Lord in his pity has done for you."
From Mark 5:1-20

While I was growing up, I had visions of grandeur regarding what I'd do with my life. I wanted to solve the problems of the world. I wanted to end wars. I wanted to fight against prejudice and injustice. I wanted to end poverty. I wanted to work with special needs children. I wanted to teach. I wanted to become a nurse...

When things began to fall into place, the path before me became less cluttered. I learned to value the seemingly mundane vocations that in reality make all of the difference in the world. A good person who deals fairly and kindly with those around her brings peace to our world. Generous couples who allow their love to spill over onto to those around them bring love to the world. Parents who nurture their children with their time and attention bring hope to this world. Caring for those we've been given to love is the most important work we can do.

O Lord, sometimes I wonder if I'm doing my loved ones or this world any good. Thank You for the precious moments with them that dispel my doubt.

Wednesday - February 1

"So he went in and said to them, 'Why this commotion and weeping? The child is not dead but asleep.'"
From Mark 5:21-43

Parents aren't supposed to bury their children... When Mike's cousin Mary became ill, her parents responded immediately. Mary's Down Syndrome had taken a toll on her heart, so every cold required a serious regimen of care to prevent further complications. Mary enjoyed a much longer life than expected as a result of her parents' diligence. Mary was twenty-two when those dreaded respiratory complications set in. This illness ended in the hospital stay that would be her last.

When we received the call, my husband was inconsolable. "This isn't right. She could have lived longer!" Mike moaned. When we drove over to Mary's home to offer our condolences, her parents greeted us with amazing news. Mike's aunt and uncle shared, "Just before Mary passed away, she told us that she was going with Jesus and she smiled." It was then that Mike accepted God's timing.

> *Gentle God, please touch the hearts of every mom and dad who has lost a child. You alone understand their grief. Console them with a generous share of peace today.*

Something To Think About...

Thursday - February 2
The Presentation of the Lord

*"When they fulfilled all the prescriptions
of the law of the Lord, they returned
to their own town of Nazareth.
The child grew and became strong, filled with wisdom,
and the favor of God was upon him."
From Luke 2:22-40*

Our first grandchild was born not long before Mike's cousin arrived from Croatia. After a years-long search, Mike had located his Croatian family. When we visited them two years earlier, Josip promised to return the favor by coming to the United States. Josip's trip coincided with Little Ellie's baptism. Mike's cousin was overwhelmed by being a part of Ellie's special day. He had guided us to the parish church where Mike's grandfather had been baptized. Now, Josip would celebrate the same ritual four generations later with Grandpa Penich's great-great granddaughter.

Josip's presence certainly enriched my appreciation of Ellie's Baptism. That link to past generations within the Penich Family emphasized the link we all share as members of God's Family.

> *Dear God, I find great comfort in the rituals we share, perhaps because I find You there. Help us to live up to the ideals that underlie our observances and to teach our children to do the same.*

Friday - February 3
St. Blaise and St. Ansgar

"Whatever place does not welcome you or listen to you, leave there and shake the dust off your feet..."
From Mark 6:7-13

I find it extremely difficult to shake the dust off of my feet. The few instances in which I've done so were the result of impending danger to someone I love. This propensity to stay connected is partially genetic and partially learned. My parents opened their door to everyone. I recall my mom saying, "I leave the door open. If people choose not to come in, it's their loss." Jesus welcomed everyone who crossed his path as well. Since I subscribe to Jesus' way of life, I try to welcome people the way Jesus did.

Still, there are people who really aren't good for us. They may not cause physical harm, but they may take a psychological or spiritual toll on us. I find that if my gut is having a strong reaction to someone, I need to listen. This doesn't necessarily mean that I need never to speak to this person again. However, it may mean that I should limit our contact as best I can. This may seem like an odd topic for a devotional page. I included it because sometimes good people think that part of "being good" is allowing ourselves to be hurt unnecessarily. Jesus couldn't disagree more.

Dear Jesus, as you walk with me, keep me safe and wise. Help me to recognize harm and guide me away from its source.

Something To Think About...

Saturday - February 4

"Why are you so terrified?
Why are you lacking in faith?"
From Mark 4:35-41

It was Monday morning when we put our son Mike on his bus. Our neighbor Ellie would keep Mike after school to wait for news. My husband and I headed to the hospital to have our second baby. I'd experienced contractions for days, so we expected a fairly quick delivery. After several hours, the nurses threw a gown at Mike and rushed me into the delivery room. They'd detected fetal distress. When he finally made his appearance, Timothy was white as a ghost. A nurse whisked our baby away without allowing me to hold him. After some whispering among the medical team, our doctor asked us not to worry, and then added that he was calling in a specialist. Mike and I prayed all night. The next morning, the doctor shared that our baby might be suffering from a grave illness that would cause some level of debilitation before taking him by age three. When the doctor left, Sister Charles who ran the lab hurried into our room. She said, "I've looked at Timothy Michael. Trust me. He will be just fine." Twenty-seven years later, I'm happy to report that Sister Charles was absolutely right!

> *O Dear God, I wept through my prayers that night, begging all the while for Tim's life. Thank you for my wonderful son —both of them!*

The Fourth Sunday - February 5
"The people were spellbound by his teaching because he taught with authority and not like the scribes."
From Mark 1:21-28

Actions speak louder than words. Ask any child, and he or she will tell you that's it's best to place your trust in the people who actually do what they say they're going to do. I think this is the reason children –and adults, too- were so taken with Jesus. They realized immediately that Jesus offered something very different from the repeated lectures of the scribes and Pharisees. The implication seems to be that the temple hierarchy wasn't convincing in their teaching because their words and actions were a mismatch. Jesus, on the other hand, spoke from the depths of his soul with no trepidation or uncertainty in his voice. I find myself most grateful for the things Jesus taught us through his life among us. Apparently I'm not alone, as I've witnessed the fruits of Jesus' teaching among his people.

I just returned from visiting my cousin. Janet was diagnosed with a brain tumor a while back. The uncertain prognosis gave her reason to engage in a serious war with the cancer. In spite of the difficult regimen of treatment, Janet has held her own. She's also maintained her extremely positive outlook. All was going fairly well until a few weeks ago when an unexpected seizure set her back. Since then, Janet's battles have been uphill all the way. Still, that underlying positive edge remains.

When I arrived, Janet lay with her eyes closed, seemingly searching for a bit of comfort in sleep. Since she seemed to be awake behind her closed eyelids, I announced my presence. "Hey!" she said with as much of a smile as she could muster. She added an "oooh" and then another in response to her discomfort. I noted her grandsons' artwork that decorated the wall in front of her. Janet couldn't help smiling when I mentioned William's and Xander's names. I filled her in on a recent family gathering and all of the prayers and good wishes that were sent her way. Again, she smiled.

Two nursing assistants interrupted our conversation. They'd been sent to move Janet from her bed to her chair. Though Janet seemed to anticipate the discomfort of this move, she responded, "Okey dokey." The move wasn't easy as Janet had been bedridden for weeks. Still, when she settled into her new position, she remarked, "I got it all." Though Janet's tumor is playing havoc with her speech, we all knew she was proud of having made it from bed to chair.

A few minutes afterward, Janet's fiancé Bob arrived. When I mentioned Bob an hour earlier, saying that he is a good man, Janet replied with a smile, "Oh, he's –yeah, he is." Bob's "hello" kiss netted only a half smile as Janet was still adjusting to the chair. Janet continued to settle in as Bob gently massaged her neck and her shoulders. Though she didn't speak, Janet seemed to become more comfortable and more peaceful. When Bob moved on to Janet's head, I shared that I'd bring my husband next time for massage lessons. Once again, Janet offered that half smile that assured us that she was indeed attending to our attention.

Our conversation was interrupted again, this time by the physical therapist. After introducing herself, she assisted Janet in moving her extremities. Poor Janet's weeks in bed had taken their toll. Still, in spite of the difficulty and the pain, Janet cooperated as best she could. She reacted to the pain by singing an "oooh" here and an "aaah" there. When I complimented her for singing rather than saying "bad" words, that smile appeared once again.

After the therapist left, Bob congratulated Janet for her effort. Then he returned to his massage, carefully and gently working each of the areas the therapist had exercised. Again, the peace returned to Janet's face.

After offering my good-bye hugs, I considered this loving couple as I walked to my car. If Bob had rented a billboard on Interstate 294 to profess to the world his love for Janet, it wouldn't have been as powerful as what I witnessed in his care for her. If Janet had commandeered a hot air balloon that sported an "I love Bob" banner and flown it over Wrigley Field, it would not have been as powerful as the smile she offered in response to Bob's name. Indeed, words aren't necessary between these two because the way they care for one another says it all.

The truth is that there is a good deal of sadness over the eventual outcome of Janet's battle. Still, the enduring love that surrounds her is far more tangible. Janet's children Jeff and Jamie, her grandsons William and Xander, her daughter-in-law Sandy, her brother Jon, sister Laura and brother-in-law Bob join her Bob in loving Janet to the max. Indeed, Janet's life is a priceless treasure that all concerned will nurture and watch over for as long as she is among them because their love is authentic.

When Jesus taught, he spoke with his words and his actions. This is what convinced those who heard him that Jesus taught with authority. More importantly, the subject matter of Jesus' teaching was love. Jesus loved more deeply and more inclusively than anyone who had come before him. Jesus offered this amazing and unconditional love as an example of God's affection for each one of us. It is this love that Bob and Janet's family extend to her. It is this love that Jesus asks of you and me on behalf of those we have been given to love.

> *Gentle Jesus, tears accompany my prayer for Janet today. Please fill her up with your love and peace as she fights this final battle. Please walk with those who love her as they remain at Janet's side.*

Monday - February 6
St. Paul Miki and Companions

"Go, therefore, and make disciples of all nations."
From Matthew 28:16-20

Kathleen was absolutely right. At the time, I was part of a very demanding post-graduate program. This was the last day of the first semester. After accepting our final assignments, Kathleen assigned a textbook to be read over winter break. I'm afraid that I didn't hide my anger very well. I told Kathleen that I'd survived the first semester only because I remained focused on celebrating Christmas with my family. Her intrusion upon this very necessary time together was unacceptable. Dedicated teacher that she was, Kathleen noted that I wasn't in high school anymore and that the assignment stood. Afterward, my classmates applauded my courage and laughed at my stupidity. "Mary, just don't read it. We're not. The day before our next class, scan the chapter titles. You'll know enough to muddle through."

I enjoyed a wonderful Christmas with my husband, my kids and the rest of the family. Afterward, good student that I was, I read the book which proved to be very helpful in my subsequent work with children and their teachers.

> *Patient God, when I baulk at the things You ask of me, open my mind to Your wisdom and my heart to Your love. Then, use the good teacher in me as You will.*

Something To Think About...

Tuesday - February 7

"She had heard about Jesus and came up behind him in the crowd and put her hand on his cloak. 'If I just touch his clothing,' she thought, 'I will get well.'"
From Mark 5:21-43

God is good! I think I first heard this phrase at least fifty years ago from my mom's aunt, Sister Gerard. My great-aunt was the sweetest, most dynamic and lively little nun. Oddly, she spent most of her career teaching at a boarding school for boys. Sister Gerard often remarked, "I've taught convicts and bishops, lawyers, janitors and butchers, and I love them all." Because Sister Gerard was eventually assigned to a parish in Chicago, we were blessed with her company often. Needless to say, her great-nieces and nephews grew to love her as much as our parents did.

Sister Gerard won several bouts with cancer through the years. With each recovery, she observed, "Sweet Jesus carried me through." At ninety-two, she discovered that her final bout was a losing battle. She smiled at me from her sickbed as she admitted, "I was a little upset that Jesus didn't cure me this time around. Then, I thought about where I'm going and I thanked Him! God is so good!"

> *Good and Wondrous God, thank you for Sister Gerard and for all of the good people who share their faith in Your Goodness with the rest of us.*

Wednesday - February 8
St. Jerome and St. Josephine

"Well did Isaiah prophesy about you hypocrites, as it is written,
'This people honors me with their lips,
but their hearts are far from me; In vain do they worship me,
teaching as doctrines human precepts.'"
From Mark 7:1-13

Lent begins two weeks from today on Ash Wednesday. This year, I've decided to get a head start on my plans for the season. Though I can still afford to lose a few pounds, I'm not going to focus on fasting. Actually, I don't think I'm going to give up anything. Instead, I'm going to be proactive and do something. This Lent, I've decided that I'm going to spend at least the same amount of time I spend in worship expressing my love for God to others. No, I'm not going to stand on street corners quoting scripture, preaching or reading my articles or this book to those who pass by. What I am going to do is to add up the hours and minutes that I spend at Mass, at prayer and at spiritual reading. Then, I'm going to figure out ways to spend at least that amount of time each day caring for others. Maybe I'll phone a lonely friend. Maybe I'll visit my Aunt Liz at the nursing home. Maybe I'll take the grandkids while my son and daughter-in-law enjoy an evening out. Maybe I'll visit the food pantries my parish supports. Maybe...

> *Dear God, it seems to me that we are at our best we when treat one another as You do. Help me to use every day of this coming Lent and all of my days to bring Your love to others.*

Something To Think About...

Thursday - February 9

*"He instructed them to
take nothing on the journey but a walking stick..."
From Mark 6:7-13*

My husband loves to travel. When our sons were young and money was tight, we still managed to eke out a driving vacation several summers. These trips involved a three-car caravan to nearby cities which boasted a baseball stadium, an amusement park and one or two additional tourist attractions. We joined my sister and her husband, friends and all of our children on these treks which proved to be great fun.

Since our sons have married and now vacation with their own families, Mike and I have been more daring with our travel. Actually, Mike has been daring, while I've bitten the bullet and allowed him to drag me along. Oddly, I always have a wonderful time once we reach our destination. The planning, packing and other preparations are what drive me crazy. Perhaps this is what Jesus was getting at when he sent out his disciples with no luggage. Perhaps he didn't want anything to keep them from making the most of their travels among us.

Thank you, Lord, for my persistent husband who continues to plan much needed times away for us in spite of my fears. Bless him with many more wonderful trips and bless me with the courage to enjoy this beautiful world and its wonderful people.

Friday - February 10, St. Scholastica

*"Jesus went into the district of Tyre.
He entered a house and wanted no one to know
about it, but he could not escape notice."
From Mark 7:24-30*

The person two places ahead of me in line remarked that he'd be wealthy if he had a dollar for every minute he spent waiting. As this man hurried out of the store, I chuckled to myself. You see, I've already found wealth in these seemingly wasted moments when nothing more than to wait is demanded of me. It is during these few minutes when the world rushes about me that I do my best thinking and my best praying. Perhaps this is the reason Jesus rose very early and stole away for quiet time as often as he could.

The scriptures tell us that Jesus' moments of peace were usually disrupted by those who desperately needed him. The same is true of you and me. Today, I'm going to try to respond as Jesus would, with patience, genuine concern and love.

> *Dearest God, I'm most grateful that others occasionally need me. Help me to respond to those in need as You would.*

Something To Think About...

Saturday - February 11
Our Lady of Lourdes

"The woman saw that the tree was good for food, pleasing to the eyes, and desirable for gaining wisdom. So she took some of its fruit and ate it; and she also gave some to her husband, who was with her, and he ate it."
From Genesis 3:1-8

One of the treasures I recall from my childhood is our large family bible. This massive volume included several separate booklets that arrived in the mail periodically. With each new booklet, my mom carefully removed the bible's cardboard cover, inserted the booklet, and replaced the cover. Afterward, my sisters and I poured over this newest addition, every page adorned with colorful pictures. When we were finished, I always returned to the first book's story of Adam and Eve, the snake and that forbidden tree. Eden looked amazing to me, at least as grand as heaven. "Why," I often asked myself, "would Adam and Eve think of disobeying God who gave them so much?"

Life in this topsy-turvy world of ours answers that question every day, doesn't it? Lucky for us that Jesus, the second Adam, and Mary, the second Eve, ignored the tempter. Through Jesus and Mary, we rediscover the gifts God intended us to enjoy forever.

Generous God, thank You for the blessings of Jesus, our Savior, and Mary, our Mother.

The Fifth Sunday - February 12

"Is not man's life on this earth a drudgery?
Are not his days those of a hireling?
He is a slave who longs for the shade,
a hireling who waits for his wages."
From Job 7:1-4, 6-7

Today, in churches everywhere around this world, the scriptures spread a generous share of melancholy. The first reading is taken from the Book of Job, our Old Testament friend who is the unfortunate victim of Satan's folly. The story tells us that after much taunting God allows Satan to test Job's faith in spite of the fact that Job is a good and just man. Satan conjures up every sort of suffering. Job loses his family, his home and his wealth. Job finds no consolation in his friends, for they blame his misfortune on some sin that Job or his forefathers must have committed. Job's life worsens with every breath. Understandably, poor Job makes no secret of his misery, and he complains incessantly to the Lord God.

This is February. My mom's birthday is February 14. She passed away nine years ago on February 20. As my thoughts turn to the bout with cancer that preceded her leave, I recall the journey that moved me to join Job in his litany of complaints. Fortunately, I also vividly recall sharing in Job's joy at the end of his story. God responded to Job and things ended well for our suffering friend. Job lived out what remained of his life at peace with himself and at peace with God.

I admit to having felt less comfortable than Job with all that had happened before the day my mom passed away. It was only afterward that I realized that things had also ended well for her. The splendid outcome of Job's earthly story was a mere shadow of the outcome that awaited him in heaven. Indeed, the same was true for my mom nine years ago, just as it is true for you and for me today.

In the second passage from the scriptures that echo in our churches today, we learn that Saint Paul handled his suffering quite differently than Job and I had. Paul's letter (1 Corinthians 9:16-19, 22-23) tells us that rather than complaining about his situation, Paul relished it. Paul immersed himself in God's Word and God's way and did everything possible to share these precious gifts with all who would listen. Like Job near the end of his story, Paul experienced a close encounter with God which overwhelmed him. As a result, Paul couldn't help himself. He preached because he found it impossible to hold the wonder of God within and because he knew that the outcome would be everything and more than he could hope for. Though you and I know the glorious end to Paul's story, the distance between that end and today sometimes makes it difficult for us to function at Paul's level of enthusiasm.

In the end, it is Jesus who extends the greatest consolation to me. Jesus immersed himself in the human experience most common to us, our suffering. Today's gospel (Mark 1:29-39) begins as Jesus leaves the synagogue with his friends. They feel very good about Jesus' work in the temple, and they're off to Peter's house to share a meal. Unfortunately, when they arrive they discover that Peter's mother-in-law is very ill. Jesus, never taken aback by such things, responds immediately. Jesus takes her hand, and Peter's mother-in-law is cured. The woman goes on to prepare the meal her guests had hoped for. Afterward, the disciples usher Jesus off to cure even more of the sick.

While this day was a miraculous one for those who met him, it had taken its toll on Jesus. The next morning, Jesus rose much earlier than the others to spend some time in prayer. Jesus went off to a deserted place to be with his Father. Through this encounter, Jesus replenished his spirit and readied himself for another day of pouring himself out for others.

Though none of us can claim to bear the weight of Jesus' concerns as he walked this earth, we do share the need to replenish our spirits. There is only so much of ourselves that we can give before our bodies and souls cry out, "Enough!" I found myself on the verge of such an outcry when my mom was sick. I absolutely could not understand what God was thinking in allowing her to decline as she did. When my husband's mother endured her last days, Mike struggled with the same question as he cared for her.

Fortunately for us both, we followed Jesus' example then, just as we try to now. We run to God when life overwhelms us. What is most astounding is that we never have to run far. God truly is everywhere when we are in need. God sat in my mom's room each day, never allowing me to leave until I acknowledged that God was managing her care. God loitered in the hallway as I left, never allowing me to pass without feeling God's affection for my mother's housemates. God hid in my car on the way home, revealing Divine Love in the lyrics of my favorite songs. God remained with me through it all. If that was not enough, each and every day, God continues to linger down the block, in my church, at our home, in grocery store lines and near a sickbed. God is everywhere, revealing compassion, mercy and love, sometimes in the smiles and support of those around us and sometimes in Person!

> *Patient God, I'm most grateful for the love that permeates every moment of my life. Even when I complain more than Job did, You overlook my foolishness and love me. Please stay with me, especially when I foolishly look away from You.*

Monday - February 13

"Wherever he made an appearance, in villages, in towns, or at crossroads, they laid the sick in the marketplaces and begged him to let them touch just the tassel of his cloak. All who touched him got well."
From Mark 6:53-56

As Lent approaches, I can't help thinking about the reason this season is so precious to me. Every year, I try to set aside these forty days much the way a couple sets aside time for a second honeymoon. If my husband Mike and I are smart enough to retreat and regroup to nurture -and sometimes recapture- our love for each other, it makes sense to do the same in our relationships with God.

Numerous scripture passages cite Jesus' popularity. Though the sick sought out Jesus at all costs, others with less obvious needs were also drawn to him. This Lent, I want to get to know that irresistible Jesus who doesn't need a thing from me, but who longs for my company just the same.

> *Gentle Jesus, I can't peer into the kind eyes that drew so many to you. Still, give me a glimpse of the heart which is blind to my sinfulness and loves me.*

Tuesday - February 14
St. Cyril and Methodius

"Why does this generation seek a sign?
Amen, I say to you, no sign will be given to this generation."
From Mark 8:11-13

I hope good Cyril and Methodius won't mind that I acknowledge Valentine's Day this February 14. As a child, I celebrated St. Valentine who bolstered the spirits of others by sending messages of love from his prison cell. February 14 is also my mom's birthday, a worthy coincidence since I learned my first lessons in love from her.

This February 14, our world gives us good reason to cling to doubt and to question the concept of love —be it in marriage, friendship, the result of parenthood, or genuine affection for our fellow humans. There are no signs in the secular world that indicate that love produces anything more than a fleeting bit of pleasure. For those who look past this secular world into the soul of our existence, the opposite is true. Indeed, love is the source —the only source- of true happiness.

> *God of Love, never let me lose sight of Your greatest gift to humankind, our ability to love one another. Thank You for all of those You have given me to love and for those who love me.*

Wednesday - February 15

*"What emerges from within a man,
that and nothing else is what makes him impure.
Wicked designs come from the deep recesses of the heart."
From Mark 7:14-23*

Frankie observed, "Nasty, nasty, nasty. He's just nasty, so don't pay him no mind!" Frankie, a fifth grader who was wise beyond her years, had mastered the art of ignoring misbehavior. Though she'd never allow one classmate to physically hurt another, Frankie ignored verbal assaults and she taught those in her company to do the same. Frankie single-handedly prevented many a playground altercation by simply walking away. While the teacher in me addressed any assault, verbal or otherwise, I truly respected this little girl's approach to getting along in this world. Apparently, so did most of her classmates who considered Frankie to be their friend. By the end of the first quarter that year, even a few potential bullies saw the light and befriended their one-time nemesis.

Precious Lord, I'm most grateful for the peacemakers among us. They counter the misdeeds of the rest of us with grace. Please fill our hearts with Frankie's desire to bring peace to this world wherever we are.

Something To Think About...

Thursday - February 16

*"'Lord,' she replied, 'even the dogs
under the table eat the family's leavings.'"
From Mark 7:24-30*

I grew up in an Irish and Italian neighborhood. Since only the tiniest drop of each bloodline flows through me, I had no preference for either group. The truth is that I envied them both, especially on St. Patrick's and St. Joseph's Days when they celebrated their heritage with great flourish. For the most part, I'm French Canadian, and there was no designated day for me to do the same. Though my family celebrates rich traditions that are the direct result of my nationality, I longed for a more colorful and universal display of our heritage.

This childhood disappointment evolved into a lifetime of effort to overlook ethnicity and the numerous other differences that often separate us. Perhaps it was providential that I spent my career working with children. My classroom provided the perfect forum in which to honor both our personal uniqueness and our common qualities.

Welcoming God, at work, in the neighborhood and even at church, we manage to separate ourselves into differing factions. Help me and all of my sisters and brothers to welcome one another into our lives as You welcome us.

Friday - February 17
The Seven Servite Founders

*"Get behind me, Satan. You are thinking
not as God does, but as human beings do."
From Mark 8:27-33*

Today is my birthday. As I write, I recall my only children's birthday party. Because money was tight in our house, I'm amazed that I actually asked for this party and that my mom agreed to host it. Though I have no recollection of our planning, I do know that my friends Trino, Adolph and Caroline joined me for ice cream, cake and games. I also recall that Trino and Adolph each handed me a shiny half dollar on their way into our flat. I don't remember any of my other guests or gifts. Still, at the time, this party was extremely important to me. I yearned for the recognition that only a "birthday boy" or "birthday girl" receives. In the end, I found myself disappointed because my shyness kept me from enjoying the limelight that I'd longed for.

When my husband surprised me with a 40th birthday party, everything was different. Though this was the last thing I wanted, it ended up being one of the nicest events of my life. This gathering of family and friends filled me up with more love than I thought I could hold.

Generous God, only You understand our deepest needs. Thank You for surprising us with these things in spite of what we think will make us happy.

Something To Think About...

Saturday - February 18

"My heart is moved with pity for the crowd. By now they have been with me for three days and have nothing to eat."
From Mark 8:1-10

My mom was an extremely hospitable woman. She opened her door to whoever knocked, offering a chair, a cup of coffee and whatever else she had to her guest. Though our kitchen table was already crowded, my mom extended her welcome to our friends who stayed for dinner occasionally. My friend Trino recently reminded me that whenever he smelled my mom's chicken and dumplings on the stove, he did everything he could to solicit an invitation to dinner. He added that he succeeded most of the time, much to his delight.

My mom's welcoming nature lives on in the rest of us. We take turns hosting our family gatherings where food and laughter are plentiful. In the best and worst of times, we break bread in good company.

Nurturing God, You feed us generously with the gifts of this earth and with one another's company. Thank You!

The Sixth Sunday - February 19

"The leprosy left him then and there, and he was cured. Jesus gave him a stern warning and sent him on his way. 'Not a word to anyone now,' he said...The man went off and began to proclaim the whole matter freely."
From Mark 1:40-45

Writing fills me up with peace. Whether the subject matter is uplifting or difficult, exploring it through the written word enhances my understanding and appreciation one thousand-fold. Still, there are times when the circumstances of this life become too much to bear. Then, even my best efforts bring me little consolation. Though I ask God's help every time I sit at my keyboard, at those times, I pray with increased urgency.

I've learned to acknowledge God's surprises in my life. Though I believe God always listens to me, God's assessment of my situation sometimes differs from my own. So it is that my prayers aren't always immediately answered during a bout with melancholy or writer's block. At these times, I reread passages from the scriptures and some of my other favorite authors with the hope that their words will do for me what I hope my words will do for others. Afterward, I head outdoors where I find God's caress is most easily felt and God's words are most easily heard. Still, I don't always return home filled with inspiration. It is then that I turn to the laundry, picking up the house or other mindless chores to distract myself from my troubles.

After all of this, I still sometimes find myself unable to

write. Indeed, this was the case this afternoon. Apparently, the recent loss of my cousin Janet is weighing heavily upon me. Though I know Janet can't possibly be happier than she is in the company of her own family and everyone else in the hereafter, her loved ones here miss her terribly. I returned to my keyboard only because quiet time is a precious commodity these days, and I need to use it well. Before returning to this manuscript, I opted to check my email. One never knows what inspiration lies out there in the world-wide web. Much to my absolute amazement, I found precisely what I needed in an email from a very dear friend...

Hi, Mary,

I just had to send you a "thank you" for your article. Each week, you touch me in a special way and truly give me "something to think about"! This week, I printed your article, but I always want to wait for a quiet moment to sit and read and absorb what you say.

The quiet moment came the other day. When I looked at my watch, I realized that you would be at Janet's funeral, and I prayed for your family. Then, I went on to read your article. I loved picturing you sitting and holding Claire and comforting her. Even though I know you were tired, it truly had to be a "God Moment" that led your thoughts to memories of Mike and Tim when they were younger.

Your words about God's mercy always nourish my soul. And your explanation or thoughts or comparison on the man who invested his faith in the fruitfulness of his seeds and his action -WOW!!! I had never really comprehended that before and it was like you served me an "extra" portion.

Now, when I'm having a not so good moment, I will remember what you wrote and remember to take extra time to talk to the God who "planted" me where I am even though there may be some "weeds" popping up in my day.

I thank God for you, your talents and the gift of your friendship!!!!!!!!!!!

HUGS and prayers,

Carol

My friend Carol is the most unassuming and gentle of God's children. She never toots her own horn, certain that any good she accomplishes is simply God working through her. Carol's life is not perfect, certainly no more so than the rest of ours. Still, she finds reason to be grateful every day.

Though Carol doesn't realize it, she has saved the day for me numerous times throughout our nineteen-year-old friendship. Somehow, Carol always manages to respond to an email, send a card or make an unexpected phone call when I need it most. Like Jesus who made all of the difference in the world to the leper he cured, Carol has made all of the difference in the world to me. Like Jesus, Carol would just as soon have me be quiet about this and send me on my way. Like the leper in today's gospel, I simply can't hold in the good news of the cure that came to me through Carol. Because of Carol, my heavy heart sings once again.

Something To Think About...

You know, our journey together through this past Advent, Christmastime and the New Year comes to a close in just a few days. As the Season of Lent approaches, I find myself wondering what I will do to bring meaning to this intimate walk to Calvary and on to Easter with Jesus. As I reconsider the impact my friend Carol has had on my life and on the lives of all who know her, I imagine for a moment what we can each do for those we've been given to love.

This coming Lent, I'll try to respond to the melancholy, the writer's block, the heavy heart, the depression, the sadness, the despair, the anger, the illness and the bad moods I encounter in those around me. Like Jesus and Carol, I'll time my efforts to meet my loved ones and not-so-loved ones needs when they need me most. Like Jesus and Carol, I'll do so without tooting my own horn or expecting anything in return. Hopefully, like Jesus and Carol, I'll make a small difference to somebody.

> *Saving God, I give You thanks for the gifts of Jesus and those like Carol who follow his way so well. No one has loved humankind as generously and as completely as Jesus. Still, those who make his loving ways their own bring Your Holy Presence to us all.*

Monday - February 20

"The Pharisees came forward and began to argue with Jesus. They were looking for some heavenly sign from him as a test."
From Mark 8:11-13

I admit to lots of anger over the suffering of those I've been given to love. Whether they are my own family members or children starving to death half a world away, I find it difficult to accept that there actually is nothing I can do to help. This is when I become like the Pharisees who badgered Jesus for signs from above to legitimize his preaching. I find myself groaning, "If only you would penetrate the hearts of those in power as you have mine!" Of course, if Jesus had revealed himself as God's Son to the Pharisees earlier on, they would have seen to his demise much sooner. Sadly, the same is true of me. If God gave me definitive signs of what I should do for those around me, I might rebel as well. God's generosity might require more than I'm prepared to give.

So it is that God leaves it to us to do the best we can as we see it. God's only assistance comes in the example of Jesus and the grace that urges us on to do as Jesus did.

Patient God, forgive my impatience with others and with You. My only concern must be to do what I can to love those I've been given to love, here and everywhere.

Something To Think About...

Tuesday - February 21, St. Peter Damian

"Jesus said to him... 'Everything is possible to one who has faith.' Then the boy's father cried out, 'I do believe; help my unbelief.'"
From Mark 9:14-29

When my Uncle Leonard passed away, Aunt Lucille was left a young window with three children ages seven and under. Still, at my uncle's funeral, the priest challenged her to make a choice. She could choose to live in the dark as result of this devastating loss or she could raise herself up to embrace the life that lay ahead. It was with great faith that Aunt Lucille chose the latter.

When my own father lay dying eight years later, my mom challenged him to let go of his worry about her and their six children and to embrace the life that lay ahead for him. It was with great faith that my dad embraced heaven that night.

If only you and I can let go of our worries and truly embrace what lies ahead every moment of every day, we will experience God's love in ways we'd never imagine or dare to hope for!

> *Loving God, thank You for walking this journey with us. Though we do our best to believe with all of our hearts, we sometimes fail. Please strengthen our faith and help our unbelief. Amen.*

for Christmastime and Winter Days

Our Journey Continues

Though the pages of this book have run out, our journey continues. We've shared these reflections, always in the company of the God of Love. Though we may not have taken notice much of the time, God has been with us all the while. The same will be true tomorrow when we begin our Lenten journeys, throughout the forty days that will us lead to Easter, and for all of our lives.

Please know that I'm most grateful to have had the opportunity to walk with you these past eighty-seven days. Your presence has meant the world to me. I hope my words have touched you in some small way.

My purpose has been and will continue to be to reveal God's presence in this world, in the circumstances of our lives and in one another. When we find the courage to open ourselves up to God's presence, we open ourselves up to the Treasure that makes this life worth living. If you've found these daily reflections helpful, please visit my blog at: marypenich.com. I post a weekly reflection much like the longer Sunday pieces which I shared in this book.

May God bless you with the best heaven has to offer, with all that you need, and with more than you would ever dare to hope for!

Mary Penich